Chatham House Papers · 28

European Interests in Latin America

Esperanza Durán

The Royal Institute of International Affairs

Routledge & Kegan Paul
London, Boston and Henley

The Royal Institute of International Affairs is an unofficial body which promotes the scientific study of international questions and does not express opinions of its own. The opinions expressed in this paper are the responsibility of the author.

First published 1985
by Routledge & Kegan Paul Ltd
14 Leicester Square, London WC2H 7PH
9 Park Street, Boston, Mass. 02108, USA and
Broadway House, Newtown Road,
Henley-on-Thames, Oxon RG9 1EN
Set by Hope Services, Abingdon and
printed in Great Britain by
Billing & Son Ltd, Worcester

Library of Congress Cataloging-in-Publication Data

Durán, Esperanza
European interests in Latin America.
(Chatham House papers; 28)
Bibliography: p.
1. Latin America—Foreign economic relations—
Germany (West)   2. Latin America—Foreign economic
relations—France.   3. Latin America—Foreign
economic relations—Great Britain.   4. Germany (West)—Foreign
economic relations—Latin America.   5. France—Foreign
economic relations—Latin America.   6. Great Britain—
Foreign economic relations—Latin America.   I. Title.
II. Series: Chatham House papers; no. 28.
HF1480.55.G3D87 1985   337.408   85-18458

ISBN 0-7102-0619-4

Contents

Abbreviations

ACP	African, Caribbean and Pacific
ASEAN	Association of South-East Asian Nations
ATP	Aid and Trade Provision
BFCE	Banque Française du Commerce Extérieur
BIS	Bank for International Settlements
CAP	Common Agricultural Policy
CCCE	Caisse Centrale de Coopération Economique
CDC	Commonwealth Development Corporation
CDU	Christian Democratic Union
COFACE	Compagnie Française d'Assurance pour le Commerce Extérieur
CSU	Christian Social Union
DAC	Development Assistance Committee
DEG	Deutsche Entwicklungsgesellschaft
DGA	Délégation Générale pour l'Armement
DOM/TOM	Départements et Territoires d'Outre Mer
DSO	Defence Sales Organization
EIB	European Investment Bank
ECGD	Export Credits Guarantee Department
FDP	Free Democratic Party
FDI	Foreign direct investment
GATT	General Agreement on Tariffs and Trade
GRULA	Grupo Latinoamericano
IDB	Inter-American Development Bank
IMF	International Monetary Fund
LAFTA	Latin American Free Trade Association
LATAG	Latin America Trade Advisory Group
LDCs	Less developed countries

Abbreviations

LLDCs	Least developed countries
NICs	Newly industrializing countries
NPT	Non-Proliferation Treaty
oda	Official development assistance
ODA	Overseas Development Administration
ODM	Overseas Development Ministry
OECD	Organisation for Economic Cooperation and Development
oof	Other official flows
OPEC	Organization of Petroleum Exporting Countries
SELA	Sistema Económico Latinoamericano
SI	Socialist International
SPD	Social Democratic Party
UNIFEX	Union pour le Financement et l'Expansion du Commerce International
UNCTAD	United Nations Conference on Trade and Development

Acknowledgments

I am grateful to the people in government departments and private organizations in Britain, France and West Germany who generously gave their time to discuss Latin American issues with me and who provided useful insights into the web of European/Latin American relations. I would also like to thank Victor Bulmer-Thomas, Hugh Holley, Shovan Ray, David Stephen and William Wallace for valuable comments on earlier drafts. Throughout the research and writing, I received friendly advice and support from Joan Pearce. This study has greatly benefited from her criticisms and comments.

I wish to extend my deep appreciation to the staff of Chatham House from whom I have received unfailing assistance and cooperation, particularly to Pauline Wickham for expert guidance, to Nigel Pearce for careful editing, to Susan Walker for all her help and to Susan Aduma for cheerful typing.

July 1985   E.D.

1 Introduction

Although formal relations between Western Europe and Latin America are long-standing, there has been little progress in exploiting their full potential. Europe has had a diminishing role in the region this century, largely because of the hegemonic influence of the United States in the western hemisphere. However, a number of circumstances in the past few decades, both within and outside the region, make it essential for Europe to rethink its relations with Latin America. Foremost among these are the relative decline of US influence in Central and South America, and Western Europe's increasingly independent role within the Atlantic Alliance.

This study has three main aims: first, to show why Latin America is an important area within the Third World in terms of its economic and political development; second, to examine current attitudes in the European Community towards Latin America and to trace their historical evolution; and, third, to point to those areas where a closer relationship could be of benefit to both regional groupings.

The first part of the paper examines the economic relations of Great Britain, France and West Germany with Latin America in the areas of trade, aid, investment and private financial involvement. The second part focuses on the political interests of these three countries in the region, and highlights the areas of possible cooperation in the future. A concluding section suggests the means by which such strengthened relations might be achieved.

The economic and political context

European economic and political interests in Latin America have been relatively unimportant up to now, and this situation seems unlikely to change significantly. The West European countries will continue to be most closely linked to their partners in the Community and to other industrialized countries such as the US and Japan, with Eastern Europe coming next in importance. However, in the context of Europe's overall relations with the Third World, there could be some advantages in closer European/Latin American cooperation.

For a number of years Latin America was regarded as an area about to take off economically. The whole region had impressive rates of economic growth, averaging 7 per cent from 1970 to 1974 and 4.9 per cent from 1975 to 1980. However, these high expectations of Latin America's role in the world economy were left largely unfulfilled, and the resulting overreaction by European and other industrialized countries has since left them without an incentive to cultivate the closer relationship that the region deserves.

Latin America became the subject of widespread international attention in 1982, when the debt crisis surfaced. The fact that the region is responsible for the bulk of the Third World international debt is significant in itself: it points to the confidence that the banking community had in the region's economic prospects and ability to repay loans; and, at the same time, it raises the question of why the crisis came about. Part of the answer is that the durability of Latin America's economic boom was untested, and bankers were unable to assess the region's prospects in the context of a world economy in recession. In addition, foreign loans were used not only to finance investment, but to cover budget and balance-of-payments deficits.

At present Latin America is experiencing its worst economic crisis since the 1930s, and the prospects for a return to its earlier impressive growth rates look bleak. Nevertheless, there are some very positive signs in the region's economic and political environment which need to be taken into account if European countries are to make a balanced assessment of the advantages that could be gained from furthering their interests there.

Before the financial crisis of 1982, the Latin American economies had grown threefold in two decades. The engine of this spectacular growth had been the manufacturing sector, followed by energy and power generation, transportation and financial services. Industrial production grew sixfold between 1950 and 1980.[1] In order to sustain this level of growth, Latin America devoted a higher proportion of its GDP to investment than did other developing regions in the world. In the late 1960s investment represented around 20 per cent of GDP, a proportion that grew to 23 per cent in the 1970s, and reached 25.8 per cent in 1981.[2]

The bulk of Latin American investment during the 1960s was financed from internal savings, US funds from President Kennedy's Alliance for Progress, and from soft loans from multilateral institutions. Foreign direct investment also played a significant role in the region's economies. Gradually, however, the character of the foreign resource flows to Latin America changed: they became less concessional, and the private (non-concessional) flows became increasingly 'debt-creating' (in the form of bank credits) rather than 'non-debt-creating' (direct investment).

There were a number of reasons for this change, the chief of which was Latin American economic nationalism. A long tradition of abuses on the part of transnational corporations regarding licensing agreements, transfer pricing (overpricing of imports of materials and technological equipment) and tax evasion, not to mention political interference in the host country's affairs, led to a growing antagonism in Latin America towards multinational enterprises. Latin American countries became convinced that their national sovereignty and control over their own economic development would be less at risk if domestic investment were financed through foreign loans rather than if an increasing share of investment were allowed to be foreign-controlled. At the same time, for private investors, transfers of capital through banks, in the form of loans, became more attractive, since it was considered less risky than investment in equity.

Traditionally foreign investment in Latin America had concentrated on public utilities and the agricultural and extractive sectors, but in the postwar period foreign direct investment was geared primarily to the manufacturing industries. In general, throughout the century, Latin America has been considered a good region for investment because of cheap and relatively well-qualified labour, high returns and growing internal markets. From the 1930s on, however, governments in the region tried to regain control of their resources by regulating the scope and activities of foreign corporations. Nationalization, the most extreme form of official action against a corporation, became a common practice, especially during the 1960s and 1970s. Between 1960 and 1976 there were 142 expropriations, aimed at 237 firms, and other, milder forms of official control of foreign enterprises were adopted by most governments in the region. Intensive legislation was introduced, including such regulatory measures as limits to equity ownership, fade-out formulas (reduction of ownership after a certain length of time), screening mechanisms and minimum export requirements.

One of the consequences of Latin America's current financial crisis has been the drastic reduction of funds for investment. The investment ratio for Latin America dropped from its peak of 25.8 per cent in 1981 to 19.6 per cent in 1983.[3] Further lending by foreign commercial banks is in rather short supply. Therefore, the Latin American governments are now trying to attract foreign capital by relaxing the regulations that they had previously initiated to control it. The Andean Pact countries (Bolivia, Colombia, Ecuador, Peru and Venezuela) are easing Decision 24, which regulates foreign investment, and even countries renowned for their strict control of foreign participation in their economies are modifying the rules without changing the law. Mexico, for instance, has recently allowed majority foreign participation, previously outlawed, in certain industrial sectors, as will be seen in more detail below. In sum, there has recently been a noticeable shift in policy in most Latin American states to allow a wider margin for multinational corporations and to provide a suitable climate for foreign investment capital. What are the attractions Latin America could hold for prospective investors?

Social indicators

It is generally agreed that during the past three decades Latin America has undergone a radical transformation in social, economic and political terms. To take social indicators first, its population grew from 200 million in 1959 to 370 million in 1983 and is expected to exceed 600 million by the year 2000. Once overwhelmingly rural, the region is now characterized by its rapid urbanization. In 1950 there were seven cities with over a million inhabitants; by 1980 there were 25 such cities, nine of them in Brazil alone; by the year 2000 they are expected to increase to about 48, ten of them with a population of over five million each. But despite this huge – primarily urban – population growth, which has been the source of some of the region's major problems, income per capita has doubled in the past twenty years, from an average of $958 in 1960 to $1,844 in 1980 (it has, however, fallen sharply since then).

Improvements in education and health have been spectacular. The percentage of children in primary schools (from six to eleven years) increased, for the whole region, from an average of 57.3 per cent in 1960 to 82.3 per cent in 1980. Advances in secondary and tertiary (technical schools and university) education were even greater: the percentage for secondary education increased from 35 to 63 per cent from 1960 to 1980, and for higher education from 6 to 26 per cent during the same period.

Compared with other low- and middle-income countries, Latin America's statistics are impressive, with an adult literacy rate of 70 per cent, nearly twice the average rate of low-income countries and almost on a par with that of the middle-income countries. The average life expectancy is 63 years, compared with averages for the low- and middle-income countries of 50 and 61 years respectively. A further indication of the advances made in health care is the decline in the infant mortality rate. This decreased in the whole of the region from an average of 105 per thousand in the period 1960–5 to 73 per thousand in the period 1975–80.

As a direct result of these changes in society, the region now displays a more diversified and flexible productive infrastructure, and has managed to build an excellent base for further industrial growth. It has a labour force with a relatively high level of education and an increasing number of workers with industrial qualifications and experience. Furthermore, labour costs are much lower than in the industrialized countries. It therefore has a comparative advantage in the production of industrial goods that do not require a high level of technological development.

Economic indicators
Given all these factors and resource endowments, one is led to ask: why has Latin America not achieved the kind of economic progress and presence in the international economy that one would expect

from the high rates of growth that it exhibited over a number of decades? One answer, from the purely economic point of view (without any attempt to include socio-political factors), is that it has adopted a mix of economic strategies which have not always been chosen with sufficient reference to developments in the world economy. The centre-piece of these was a protectionist import-substitution policy, which was later accompanied by attempts at regional economic integration and a drive towards export manufactures.

The import-substitution strategy, adhered to by most countries in the region during the 1950s and 1960s, whatever its merits, seems to have been particularly untimely given the postwar boom in international trade in manufactures, from which the region cut itself off. It thereby missed an opportunity that its early start in industrial development (dating back to the late nineteenth and early twentieth century) might have given it. A more export-oriented pattern of development was gradually adopted in the late 1960s and early 1970s, and a marked increase in the exports of manufactured and semi-manufactured products in Brazil, Mexico and Argentina was noticeable during the 1970s. Thus, for example, in 1970, coffee represented 34 per cent of Brazil's total exports, whereas manufactures accounted for only a quarter of the total; by 1980 coffee had dropped to 12.5 per cent, and industrial goods had climbed to 57 per cent.

Latin America's trade performance in recent decades has been poor, and its share in world trade has been steadily declining, beyond what the more recent deterioration in global conditions might explain. Indeed the region's share of total world exports has more than halved: from 12.4 per cent in 1950 to a meagre 6.1 per cent by 1981.[4] On the import side, the region's share of the world total has naturally also declined, although by a smaller proportion: from 10.1 per cent in 1950 to 6.3 per cent in 1981. However, there has been an increasing diversification of Latin American exports. Traditionally Latin America has been an exporter of primary products and raw materials and an importer of manufactures and capital goods. Although this pattern broadly persists, there has been a steady growth in the manufactured goods exported by the region, especially those goods which are labour-intensive, such as automobile parts and electrical and non-electrical machinery. Thus in 1965 manufactures and semi-manufactures accounted for 8.5 per cent of Latin America's exports; by 1970 the proportion had grown to 15 per cent, and by 1978 to 26 per cent.[5] Admittedly, the term 'manufactured product' is often rather loosely defined, but these percentages do at least indicate the region's growing industrial sophistication. In the specific category of road motor vehicles (for which the bulk of production is still in the industrialized countries) the figures are especially encouraging, with Brazil and Mexico accounting for 47 per cent of total exports from developing countries.

Nevertheless, Latin America's strength in trade is still in primary products and raw materials, and its importance as a net exporter of food should not be underestimated. Although the region is still a net importer of cereals, dairy products and eggs, food exports exceed imports in five categories: meat; fruit and vegetables; sugar and honey; animal and vegetable oils; and coffee, tea and cocoa. Coffee is still the region's most important single export, Brazil accounting for 22.3 per cent of the world total and Colombia for 18.9 per cent. But its share in other items is also considerable: in 1980 Argentina exported 12.9 per cent of the world total of meat and 12.2 per cent of cereals; Chile 15.7 per cent of the world's copper; and Brazil 21.4 per cent of iron ore and concentrates, 15.5 per cent of animal feedstuffs and 8.4 per cent of tobacco. In the oil market, Latin America has three major exporters: Venezuela, Ecuador and Mexico. Mexico is not a member of OPEC, but the other two are, and indeed Venezuela's Juan Pablo Pérez Alfonzo, at that time Minister of Mines and Hydrocarbons, was one of the leading forces behind the creation of OPEC.

As for imports, these are an even more telling indication of the region's significance in international trade. In 1980 imports for Latin America and the Caribbean amounted to $120.9 billion (c.i.f.); they increased to $125.3 billion in 1981, the peak year; and they dropped to $105.5 billion in 1982.[6] To this it should be added, as a last general remark, that Latin America's economic development is uneven, the four large 'regional powers' — Brazil, Mexico, Argentina and Venezuela — showing the greatest dynamism in terms of industrial growth and size of GNP per capita.

In short, despite the recent crisis and continuing economic slump, the trend in Latin America is one of growth. With the resumption of 'normality', the importance of the region must inevitably increase, whether measured by population and urbanization, production and wealth, or interaction with the rest of the world.

Political indicators

Traditionally Latin America has been regarded as being in the exclusive sphere of influence of the United States. Recently, however, the actions of the Latin American countries, individually and collectively, have led to a revised notion of the region as a relatively independent and increasingly important political force.

Collectively, the Latin American countries have played a leading role in Third World international politics. They were the force behind the creation of the Group of 77 in the early 1960s, and of the Group of 24 in 1972. The former (with 122 members at present) is the principal organ by means of which Third World countries can articulate and promote their economic and political interests vis-à-vis the industrialized world in various international organizations, such as the United Nations General Assembly and the United Nations Conference on Trade and Development (UNCTAD). The Group of 24 carries out a similar function with the International Monetary Fund (IMF) and the World Bank. The real achievements of the Group of 77, which include the Generalized System of Preferences (GSP) and the Common Fund for Commodities, are isolated but important, and it is certainly becoming a significant actor in international negotiations.

In the field of disarmament, Latin America has played a very important international role. The idea that a denuclearized Latin America would contribute to the achievement of worldwide nuclear non-proliferation led a group of Latin American leaders to initiate negotiations which culminated in the Treaty of Tlatelolco in 1967. This treaty, which preceded the Non-Proliferation Treaty (NPT) of 1968, turned Latin America into the first inhabited nuclear-free zone. There are still some loopholes in the Treaty of Tlatelolco, and some Latin American countries have not fully adhered to it. (Most of these have also refused to become signatories of the NPT.) This has become a source of international concern, which points to the importance of the region in the very sensitive fields of nuclear proliferation and international security.

Individually, the Latin American countries have made great progress in recent years in their development towards democracy. In the past five years or so, military dictatorships in Peru, Ecuador, Bolivia, Argentina and Uruguay have given way to democratic regimes, and a similar process has occurred, if in a special way, in Brazil. Electoral practices as a means of choosing national governments are becoming more and more common, especially in Central America, where — with the exception| of Costa Rica — dictatorial regimes have been the rule. Relatively free elections have been taking place in Honduras, El Salvador and Nicaragua and will follow shortly in Guatemala. Admittedly, democracy in Latin America does not conform with the ideal western liberal model, but the spread of democratic practices throughout the region is nevertheless a sign of a growing political awareness at grass-roots level which will help strengthen political stability and ensure the existence of legitimate governments.

Finally, there is the subject of religion, in which Latin America has played a pioneering role. A predominantly Catholic region, it has been the leader of what has been considered the most important theological movement of the postwar period: the theology of liberation. The central features of this movement are the blending of religion and politics, and the concept of organization to improve the lot of the poor. The activist clergy who support the theology of liberation seek to bring the Church closer to the people's needs, particularly those of the very poor. They have encountered stern opposition from the Vatican, but their ideas have found an echo all over the world and have greatly influenced Protestant Churches. Thus the World Council of Churches has adopted a Protestant version of liberation theology as an ideological framework. The theology of liberation could have an important influence in the future, not only on political change in Latin America, but in the wider context of relations between the region and other Catholic areas and countries in the world, not least in Europe.

Europe's relations with Latin America

Relations between Europe and Latin America are hailed for their promise and growing importance. However, hard facts and achievements have not yet kept pace with the political pronouncements and expressions of goodwill made by political leaders in both regions over

9

the past decade and a half, or with the assessments made by many analysts. It has been argued that in the context of a changing international system, with the loosening of the bipolar structure and the emergence of new poles of political and economic power, each of the two regions offers the other considerable attractions as a prospective partner.

There are fundamental affinities between the two groups of countries which could eventually facilitate greater political and economic links. For one thing, the two regions lie firmly in the western world, in terms both of cultural background and of politico-economic allegiance. Perhaps there is no other area in the Third World with which Europe has so many religious, cultural and idiosyncratic similarities. The existence in both regions of mixed economies is another feature held in common. On the political front, too, continental Europe and Latin America display surprisingly similar political cultures in some respects; no other region in the Third World has such long-established political movements of European origin, such as Christian and Social Democracy.

Although Spain and Portugal were the main colonial powers in Latin America, the region established strong links (mainly economic, but also political) with other European countries. From the post-independence period of the majority of Latin American countries (roughly in the second decade of the nineteenth century) to the beginning of World War I, the importance of these relations steadily grew, especially in terms of trade and investment. For Latin America, Europe became a provider of capital to finance the governments of the new republics and the fledgling economies of the region, mainly through investment in government bonds, public utilities and the agricultural and mining sectors. For Europe, Latin America was a growing market for its exports and a relatively secure supplier of raw materials. Up to 1913 Britain was the largest foreign investor in the region, far outstripping the United States in much of Latin America (though not in Mexico and Central America). It was only after World War I, and particularly in the period following the Great Depression, that the US started to displace Europe as the main source of foreign investment. After World War II, the − by then − overwhelming economic and political influence of the US in Latin America, together with the fact that Europe was tied up in its own reconstruction, impeded the development of a closer relationship between Latin America and Europe. Bilateral relations between countries in the two regions remained limited but cordial.

The creation of the European Economic Community, and the progressive process of integration of the European countries into it, introduced a new dimension in European/Latin American relations. Europe now had a collective mechanism with which to deal with the area. However, this new collective approach has not yielded significant results, either in bringing the two regions closer economically or in improving the quality of relations.

After the signing of the Treaty of Rome in 1957, the members of the newly established European Community sent the Latin American countries a 'memorandum of intention' declaring their aim to establish close relations and cooperation with the area, and specifying that the Community's preference for internal trade would not affect commercial prospects between the two regions. The Latin American countries, seeing a certain similarity in their own situation to that of the Europeans, began to consider economic integration among themselves, and in 1961 they set up the Latin American Free Trade Association (LAFTA).

Still tied to their colonial past, the members of the EC extended preferential treatment first to their former colonies in Africa, through the Yaoundé Conventions (1964, renewed in 1969), and subsequently to other former colonies in the Pacific and the Caribbean, through the Lomé Conventions of 1975, 1979, and 1984. This was resented by the Latin American countries, which were finding it increasingly difficult to export their agricultural products because of the high level of protectionism resulting from the Common Agricultural Policy (CAP). The commercial agreements with the ACP (African, Caribbean and Pacific) countries was an added blow, because their products were very similar to those that Latin America exported to the EC (namely petroleum, coffee, cocoa, sugar, iron ore, blister copper and cotton). The EC responded to Latin American representatives by asking them to submit a list of their exports which would be affected by European protectionism and a statement on the long-term trade objectives of the region. The Latin American countries, through their diplomatic representatives in Brussels, issued the 'memorandum of 1966', in which

11

they responded to these questions and proposed the creation of a joint commission of Latin American and EC representatives. There was no European response to this memorandum, and official contacts between the two regions came to a standstill. Then, in July 1970, the Latin American countries took the initiative and met under the aegis of the Special Committee for Latin American Coordination (CECLA)* to issue the Declaration of Buenos Aires. This document expressed Latin America's concern about the region's declining trade with the EC, called for a renewal of official contacts and reiterated Latin America's wish to establish a permanent joint commission. This time the EC responded, and a regular series of meetings between the group of Latin American ambassadors in Brussels (GRULA) and EC representatives was initiated.

However, the Brussels dialogue does not seem to have contributed significantly to creating closer relations. The 'dialogue of the deaf', as one observer has dubbed it, has faced a number of problems and has not had a continuous existence. These problems fall into three broad categories: first, the difficulty in achieving agreement even on the issues which *can* be discussed, let alone those which fall outside the competence of the EC and are matters of national policy; second, a lack of expertise (and interest) among Latin American ambassadors (and EC officials) in discussing certain highly technical issues, such as those concerning trade negotiations and investment decisions; and, third, the marginal importance of Latin America for the EC, and the inability of Latin American countries to give any concrete proof of the advantages that closer cooperation could offer.

In view of the lack of progress in Brussels and in any collective Latin American approach to Europe, the EC concentrated instead on bilateral relations with the major Latin American countries. Non-preferential trade agreements were signed with four Latin American states (not surprisingly, the 'big three' were included): Argentina in 1971, Uruguay in 1973, Brazil in 1973 and Mexico in 1975. Interestingly enough, the EC also signed an agreement with the Andean Pact in 1983, and an agreement with Central America is under discussion.

*An *ad hoc* group formed in 1963 to coordinate the Latin American countries' attitudes towards issues which would be dealt with at the first meeting of UNCTAD.

The fact that the Andean and Central American countries have an institutionalized integrated organization illustrates the point that the EC finds it easier to deal with groups of countries that can present a common front.

In 1979 there were efforts to inject some life into the moribund Brussels dialogue. The GRULA proposed a new joint statement of cooperation between the two groupings and an increase in the number of meetings. The EC expressed reservations about the list of issues suggested for negotiation by the GRULA, and argued that some of the subjects would fall into national rather than Community policy. It issued a counter-proposal that the dialogue be limited to economic issues: trade, investment and transfer of technology. There was agreement on this, but there were other stumbling-blocks, which on two occasions led to the suspension of the dialogue. First, in 1979, there was the admission of Cuba to the GRULA, which was opposed by some EC states, even more so after the Soviet invasion of Afghanistan. The decision to admit Cuba was evidence of poor judgment. Cuba's role in the GRULA would of necessity have been rather limited, since, along with the other countries of the Soviet bloc, Cuba does not recognize the EC as a political entity and therefore does not have an accredited ambassador to the EC. The issue was settled in 1981, when the Latin Americans decided that the GRULA would only comprise those Latin American ambassadors in Brussels who were accredited to the EC, which effectively eliminated Cuba's membership.

The second obstacle to the continued existence of the Brussels dialogue was the South Atlantic conflict. The Latin American countries, as a protest against the sanctions imposed on Argentina by EC member states in a gesture of solidarity with the UK, suspended the dialogue. Although it has since been informally renewed, there does not seem to be much hope of reviving this ailing channel of communication.

It is fair to say that the EC might feel better able to negotiate with the region if all the Latin American countries would for this purpose overcome the disparities among themselves (in terms of levels of development, resource endowment, political outlook) and act as a unified and coordinated whole, as, for instance, ASEAN does, or such subregional Latin American groupings as the Andean Pact or the Central American Common Market. The creation of SELA (Sistema

Económico Latinoamericano) in 1975 was an attempt on the part of Latin American countries to achieve this sort of integrated system. SELA was to act as a permanent organ of consultation and co-ordination which would provide a mechanism for collective negotiations and the adoption of common economic and political positions within international organizations and vis-à-vis third countries. It has been particularly concerned with doing research into the state of European/Latin American relations, with the aim of seeking a rapprochement between the two regions.[7] The SELA Council has also tried to play its part in improving Latin American relations with the EC: in September 1983 it decided to press for the resumption of the dialogue at ambassadorial level.

After the deterioration in European/Latin American relations, at all levels, which followed the Falklands conflict, the European Commission attempted to revive and strengthen the links between the two regions. It was decided, so far as budgetary constraints would allow, that the Community's involvement in Latin America should be upgraded by, first, making the extra-Community financing facilities of the European Investment Bank (EIB) available to Latin America; second, giving special importance to industrial, scientific, and energy cooperation as well as to trade promotion; third, increasing significantly the training programmes for Latin American nationals; and, last, intensifying efforts in the fields of information and cultural exchanges. The Commission justified paying this increased attention to Latin America by pointing out that it would be in the Community's own interest to do so: 'The resulting rapprochement between Latin America and Europe would in its turn inevitably strengthen the Community's position in the world.'[8]

Another point of contact between the EC and Latin America is the institutionalized one of the Inter-Parliamentary Conferences. These were established as a result of the Declaration of Buenos Aires, and are regular meetings between representatives of the European Parliament and the Latin American legislatures. The aim is to discuss economic and political issues of mutual concern, mainly trade and cooperation, democratic developments in the region and human rights issues.

In addition to these interregional contacts, nine EC countries individually participate in an important Latin American institution:

the Inter-American Development Bank.* IDB membership has yielded considerable economic benefit to some European countries in that it qualifies them to bid in procurement awards for IDB projects. The sums involved in these procurement contracts are often sufficient to outweigh their subscription to the Bank. The IDB has also been important for Europe in so far as it has facilitated commercial links between European and Latin American business organizations and provided a source of reliable information on economic and social developments in the region.

In order to assess the prospects for closer relations it is important to try to identify European interests in Latin America. However, it is quite impossible to regard European interests as a unified whole. Even if attention is restricted to the European Community as the unit of analysis, the interests of its member states in Latin America vary considerably, as do the nature of their involvement and their approaches to policy. It is therefore necessary to conduct the discussion with reference to a specific set of countries within the group, and here three of the more influential members of the EC have been chosen: Great Britain, France and the Federal Republic of Germany. There is a fourth large member of the EC, Italy, and two other European countries of importance in this context, Spain and Portugal, all of which have substantial links with Latin America deriving from demographic or historical factors, but some limits to the study must be set. Moreover, the inquiry has been conducted from a comparative perspective, as opposed to concentrating, as is usual, on the EC as a whole or on one of its members alone. Identification of common threads and similarities, and of contrasts, casts mutual light on each country's approach to Latin America and provides a useful framework for analysing the state of, and prospects for, their relations. Also, comparisons are important when assessing the areas of possible cooperation or conflict in which concerted action by these European countries might more clearly lead to changes and help bring these two distant regions closer together economically and politically.

From a global perspective, Britain, France and West Germany relate to Latin America along two main axes: the East/West conflict and the

* Belgium, Denmark, France, Germany, Italy, the Netherlands, the UK, Spain and Portugal.

North/South dialogue. In the context of the former, the USA's special relationship with Latin America is of paramount importance. European perceptions of the region and actions towards it have to be considered in the light of US reactions and their effects on the Atlantic Alliance. Admittedly, US hegemonic dominance in Latin America has slackened considerably, and these three European countries seem to have contributed to and taken advantage of this fact. They have for instance successfully challenged the USA's overwhelming presence in certain economic fields, such as the arms trade in the case of France or the sale of nuclear technology in the case of West Germany. In the political sphere, however, West European countries have by and large been more cautious in challenging US hegemony in Latin America, notwithstanding the fact that some have not always lined up with US positions and policies, especially in crisis areas or situations such as Central America or Grenada.

In the North/South context, Latin America is something of a special case for Europe. Although undoubtedly part of the South, its level of industrialization in general, and the per capita incomes in most of its countries, disqualify it from being a top priority region for aid as such. In addition, its level of economic activity and the size of its market make it an area where trade and business opportunities attract European attention. In this respect it is West Germany that has been most successful at trading with and investing in the region.

In terms of overall importance, Latin America is an area of low priority for all three of the European countries being examined, a fact which can have an interesting implication: the party in power can more readily carry out policies in line with its political ideology or preferences, without having to worry too much about major risks or dangers. One such example is the French/Mexican communiqué recognizing the rebel forces in El Salvador; another, Britain's intermittent relations with Pinochet's regime in Chile. But, equally, and precisely because Latin America is an appropriate area for political or economic experimentation, policy tends to be volatile, and in fact none of these three countries has a coherent long-term policy towards the region.

Given the size and relative proximity of Latin America, it is tempting to look for explanations for the strikingly limited interest

Western Europe has taken in it. In the case of Britain and France, one important explanation seems to lie in their colonial past. Countries, even superpowers, have a limited amount of attention and energy they can devote to other countries. The British and French pattern of relations, as far as relations with the South are concerned, thus reflect the two countries' historical links with their past possessions, which do not include the bulk of Latin America. As an illustration of this, in the case of Latin America itself, the few former colonies and territorial possessions of Britain and France are, by Latin American standards, relatively small and unimportant, and yet they are the recipients of a disproportionate share of British and French trade, aid, investment and political attention to the region. By the same token, it can be argued that Germany's lack of ex-colonial involvement has left it free, in a historical sense, to establish more substantial links with Latin America, and it is a fact that Germany's political and economic presence in the region as a whole far exceeds that of its European partners.

2 Trade

Europe's trade with Latin America is not very significant when compared with its interests in other areas of economic activity, such as invest-ment, or indeed when compared with its exposure to Latin American debt. Nevertheless, there seems to be an increasing awareness in Europe that Latin America could present fruitful commercial opportunities, an attractive possibility in view of the increasingly competitive nature of international trade. The United States, however, clearly still has the advantage over Europe, since its geographical proximity to many Latin American countries makes it the obvious main extraregional trading partner for many of them, despite numerous statements by Latin American leaders on the wisdom of diversifying their trade relations.

Of the three countries to be examined in this paper, West Germany is the one which has been most successful in penetrating Latin America commercially, but recently even Germany's trade with the region has been negatively affected by Latin American financial troubles. Another obstacle to increased trading links between the two regions is the charge by both sides of growing protectionism for the other's products. The Latin Americans have resented the preferential treatment granted to the ACP countries under the Lomé Conventions. Europeans claim that they have extended the Generalized System of Preferences to cover a number of products from Latin America, but that the Latin American countries have not taken full advantage of this facility. Europeans also emphasize that Latin America continues to have a trade surplus with Europe.

Overview

When proponents of closer relations between Latin America and

Western Europe try to highlight the possibilities of a rapprochement, they commonly point to the complementarity of the two regions with respect to trade: Europe is an important exporter of capital goods needed by Latin America, and the latter is a traditional exporter of raw materials in great demand in the Old World. For Europe, Latin America is an open market with great potential, while for Latin America, Europe could be a viable alternative partner that will enable it to diversify its economic relations, heavily concentrated on the US, and to expand its trade. In sum, greater commercial links between the two regions would be mutually beneficial.

Why, then, have such relations not developed? A look at the trade figures for the past decade reveals that the complementarity argument, though perhaps strong in theory, has not been translated into practice: trade between the two regions is not very significant in either regional or bilateral terms. Thus, for instance, German exports to Latin America amounted to DM 11.5 billion in 1980, or 3.3 per cent of total exports. In contrast, 79 per cent of all German exports went to (and 75 per cent of imports came from) industrialized countries, for which complementarity arguments would be harder to make. It is a similar picture with France and the United Kingdom. For France, imports in 1981 from Latin America accounted for a mere 2.8 per cent of total imports, with exports taking a 2.6 per cent share of the corresponding total. For Britain, after a very respectable 10 per cent in the 1950s, and 4 per cent in 1970, exports to Latin America accounted for only 2.0 per cent of total exports in 1980, and 1.7 per cent in 1982; its imports from the region accounted for 2.1 and 2.0 per cent in the two years indicated. Similarly, German exports to Latin America, which, as noted above, were 3.3 per cent of the German total in 1980, dropped to 2.6 per cent in 1982, compared with 3.1 per cent in 1981. Admittedly, the figures for the early 1980s reflect the immediate impact of the debt crisis on Latin America's capacity to import, but the general picture of the relative lack of importance of Latin America as a trading partner for Europe remains the same.

When one looks at Europe as a whole, the picture shows a broadly similar trend. The EC of Ten's collective share in Latin America's foreign trade has been steadily declining: from 30.9 per cent for Brazil in 1972 to 13.6 per cent in 1981; and from 19.6 to 12.5 per cent for

Mexico over the same period. It is interesting to note that Argentina is an exception in this regard, as is Germany. The EC's share in Argentina's trade declined through the 1970s (as it did in Brazil's and Mexico's) but still remained consistently high, only dropping from 31 per cent in 1972 to 25.9 per cent in 1980, well above the US and Canadian performance throughout the decade. Meanwhile Germany, by virtue of its greater share of world trade, and the fact that a bigger proportion of its trade is with Latin America, has had a much more considerable trade presence in the region than France or Britain. German exports to each of the three Latin American countries under consideration, while still relatively modest, exceed the combined exports of France and the UK, in some cases very comfortably so. Table 2.1 gives the general picture. One striking feature is Mexico's

Table 2.1. Some industrialized countries' share (%) in selected Latin American countries' total imports: 1972, 1981

Importing country	FRG		France		UK		EC		US	
	1972	1981	1972	1981	1972	1981	1972	1981	1972	1981
Argentina*	11.6	9.3	3.1	3.6	6.1	3.3	31.0	25.9	22.6	22.6
Brazil	13.7	4.9	3.9	2.7	n.a†	n.a†	30.9	13.6	28.0	16.3
Mexico	9.0	4.9	2.8	2.4	3.2	1.8	19.6	12.5	60.5	63.9

*1981 column figures are for 1980.
†Not one of the top ten sources of Brazil's imports.

Source: 1981 UN Yearbook of International Trade Statistics (New York, 1982).

very high trade dependence on the US. For a country of Mexico's level of development and industrialization, this dependence on one market is quite extraordinary. Although this case is unusual, it shows how essential it is for Mexico and the rest of the Latin American countries to diversify their trade.

Trade competition among the industrial nations is becoming increasingly harsh. The world recession has had a particularly negative impact on the international trading system: markets have closed, and a wave of protectionist measures has spread in both developed and developing countries. In this context of growing competition, the decline of European exports to Latin America is a cause for concern, and it is evident that Europe would greatly value more significant commercial relations with the region. There has been an intensive drive in Britain, France and Germany to achieve this, by such means as visits by highly placed officials to the area (recently British and French trade ministers, Paul Channon and Mme Edith Cresson) and diplomatic and investment initiatives related to trade considerations (increased use of fairs and trade centres, and the use of export incentives). The emphasis on the use of trade promotion instruments varies according to the country and depends on the overall commercial and industrial policies of each, as well as on the role and degree of government intervention in the economy.

Among the trade promotion instruments, government credit facilities – often subsidized – have become increasingly important, since credit is central to the capital goods market, on which European exports to Latin America have concentrated. Increasing competition in the extent of official support for export credits led the member countries of the OECD Trade Committee to reach in 1976 an informal 'Consensus' on minimum interest rates and down payments, maximum maturities, and how much local-cost financing was to be permitted for export credits with official support for two or more years. Permitted interest rates and maturities would vary depending on which category of country they were granted to: the lowest interest rates and longest maturities were accorded to buyers from relatively poor countries, with terms becoming progressively closer to those for commercial credits for intermediate and relatively rich countries. In 1978 the Consensus was formalized into an Arrangement on Guidelines for Officially Supported Export Credits. After the signature of the Arrangement, market interest rates in most countries began to increase markedly, thus making the minimum interest rates permitted by the Arrangement even more subsidized than before. This led to a new agreement being reached in 1982 which not only increased interest rates and shortened repayment periods, but revised the classification of countries, many relatively poor countries graduating into the intermediate category. This measure affected most of the Latin American countries, even those with a relatively low per capita income such as Ecuador, the Dominican Republic and Jamaica.[1]

The role of the agencies in charge of providing export credits and guarantees is crucial. Without credit facilities Latin American countries would not be able to import European — or other — capital goods. The principal agencies in charge of providing export finance and guarantees are: in Britain, the Export Credits Guarantee Department (ECGD); in France, the Compagnie Française d'Assurance pour le Commerce Extérieur (COFACE); and, in Germany, Hermes and Treuarbeit.

Although the criteria for granting export credits and guarantees are strictly speaking commercial and will depend on the credit-worthiness of the importing country, in fact they can often acquire political undertones. Thus, for instance, Cuba has had difficulty in obtaining credit and insurance facilities on a number of occasions. In 1965, COFACE held back insurance for credits from a French company that had been contracted to build a fertilizer plant in Cuba. The delay was used to put pressure on Castro to indemnify the French companies that had been nationalized. The French tactic failed, since Cuba was able to get the fertilizer plant from Britain.[2] More recently, export insurance from Germany to Cuba was not forthcoming on account of the 'Berlin clause' which Bonn attaches to bilateral trade agreements, making them extensive to Berlin. Cuba, which has a different interpretation of the ambiguous status of Berlin, finds this clause unacceptable as a matter of principle, and because of this, the German government refuses to renegotiate its bilateral debt with Cuba and does not offer cover for trade with the island.[3]

In the case of the UK, trade promotion has been carried out through the British Overseas Trade Board, which, among its sixteen Area Advisory Groups, has one devoted to Latin America. The purpose of these groups in general has been to advise the British government on all aspects of Britain's export trade, and to be a source of information to British exporters on opportunities for increasing their overseas sales and investments. The Latin America Trade Advisory Group (LATAG), like those groups in charge of other geographical areas, informs the Department of Trade and Industry, the FCO, the Bank of England and the Export Credits Guarantee Department on all aspects of trade with Latin America. It works separately from, but parallel to, the British embassies and disseminates information about industrial development and needs in Latin America, and on the export opportunities British industrialists might take advantage of in the region.

Since British exports to Latin America reached an all-time low in 1982 (1.7 per cent of total exports went to Latin America), there has been a conscious effort to improve Britain's position as an exporter. Export promotion efforts have been geared towards identifying the sectors in which British industry is competitive, and providing the information necessary to make these sectors aware of the opportunities available in Latin America. One important purpose of this export promotion effort is to break down commonplace prejudices about Latin America and to emphasize to potential exporters that not only does Latin America have a great potential for economic growth despite the gloomy shadows cast by the debt crisis, but Latin American importers do pay their bills. In other words, the debt crisis should not turn British exporters away from an otherwise dynamic market.

The plan to boost British exports to Latin America was based on Britain's comparative advantage and international competitiveness in several sectors of industry, and as a starting-point six target countries were chosen. The industries on which efforts were concentrated for export promotion were the chemical industry, electrical power machinery, specialized machinery for particular industries, and scientific instruments. The countries in Latin America which were selected on account of their creditworthiness and development potential were Brazil, Chile, Colombia, Mexico, Peru and Venezuela. This strategy of selective export promotion has shown a good performance so far, since in the short term sales of the selected British lines of export to the selected Latin American countries have had a marked increase.

France, whose economic policies have been traditionally regarded as *dirigiste*, has followed an export policy which involves open government participation in sales promotion. Thus, while the British government is active indirectly through LATAG in promoting exports to Latin America, the French strategy for increasing trade with the region has been directed from above. France's Minister for External Trade, Mme Edith Cresson, has outlined the new French policy to increase its exports in the face of economic austerity and the import squeeze that the Third World has had to impose: it is to move away from negotiating

23

large contracts for major projects, and to concentrate on promoting the export of consumer goods and industrial equipment. The financial crisis in Latin America has come as a sharp indication that the heyday of 'les grands contrats' may be over, and that they will become the exception rather than the rule. The uncertain future of the nuclear contract between Germany and Brazil, discussed in more detail below, illustrates this well. Thus, with new economic constraints in the importing countries, the priority of concentrating export efforts on large quantities of standard products rather than on a few large contracts has become evident. However, in certain cases, where trading relations have been traditionally close, France has managed to maintain a share of the big contracts. In Mexico, for instance, where the cuts in imports have been drastic, France has been able to win orders for two container ships, the contract for the construction of a fish-canning factory and official Mexican agreement that France should continue to build the Mexico City underground.[4]

A common feature of European trade with Latin America is that it is heavily concentrated on certain countries. In the case of West Germany, trade is conducted mainly with Brazil and Mexico. German/Brazilian imports and exports used to be of roughly the same magnitude (around a billion dollars per annum), but since 1977 the balance has been progressively more favourable to Brazil. Indeed in 1982 it reached a very unfavourable level for Germany, since in that year Brazil exported to Germany approximately twice what it imported (see Table 2.2). The Brazilian debt crisis must have weighed heavily on German exporters.

This upward trend in the Brazilian trade surplus with Germany, as indeed with the OECD group as a whole, has been at least partially due to the country's heavy dependence on imported oil. Whereas imports from Iraq and Saudi Arabia, Brazil's current second and third most important trading partners, accounted for just 3.7 per cent of total Brazilian imports in 1970, that figure grew to 15 per cent by 1975 and to a massive 25 per cent in 1980.[5] This rise was partly reflected in Brazil's increasing foreign debt over the same period, as has been widely asserted. But also, a heavy deficit with one group of countries must of necessity have meant passing on an equally heavy surplus to other countries, including Germany.

Table 2.2 French, German and British trade with Latin America, 1980–2 (current US $ mn)

	France Imports			France Exports			Federal Republic Imports			Federal Republic Exports			United Kingdom Imports			United Kingdom Exports		
	1980	1981	1982	1980	1981	1982	1980	1981	1982	1980	1981	1982	1980	1981	1982	1980	1981	1982
Argentina	431	400	205	297	265	254	1255	1053	617	709	496	576	402	331	68	166	271	107
Brazil	699	578	600	1192	1258	1159	1541	1021	890	1607	1529	1727	507	352	278	689	739	777
Mexico	545	646	419	422	733	736	1217	1477	1042	319	302	147	437	422	289	259	144	166
Venezuela	360	399	459	361	560	337	600	552	566	378	362	492	306	254	260	273	249	246
Chile	190	220	111	277	237	207	277	323	199	602	465	492	130	126	99	294	180	195
Colombia	169	156	115	146	117	74	290	259	265	690	567	609	97	91	88	80	69	60
Peru	67	134	78	84	94	114	192	387	243	170	115	139	108	101	69	180	132	162
Bahamas	11	15	74	71	7	43	10	47	14	368	26	7	180	367	45	137	61	31
Guadeloupe	466	405	401	92	90	82	16	13	11	2	1	–	7	3	6	9	–	–
Haiti	18	23	14	37	17	20	10	9	11	10	10	13	7	4	7	2	3	5
Jamaica	10	10	10	1	6	–	16	24	23	7	6	5	77	86	97	222	231	163
Martinique	442	379	392	71	100	108	17	12	12	11	5	9	6	2	4	1	1	–
Total*	3617	3698	2985	3251	3360	3237	5611	5474	3938	5734	4571	4827	3112	3030	2040	2911	2634	2368

*Total does not include Venezuela.
Source: IMF, International Trade Statistics (Washington, D.C.).

The commercial relationship with Mexico is more advantageous to Germany than the one with Brazil. The German trade surplus with Mexico is quite substantial: in 1981 Mexico imported five times the value of its exports to Germany; in 1982 the gap narrowed, but by less than 20 per cent. In absolute terms, however, as was seen in Table 2.1, the lion's share of Mexico's trade is still with the US.

In addition to holding a very important position in these two countries' trade, Germany has a strong commercial foothold throughout the region. It is among the five leading exporters to the most important Latin American countries, being the third largest in 1980 for Argentina, Chile, Colombia, Ecuador, Guatemala, Mexico, Peru and Venezuela, and the fifth most important exporter to Bolivia, the Dominican Republic and Haiti. However, it is not among the leading exporters to any of the Central American countries (with the exception of Guatemala) or to Paraguay. The implication of this is that Germany's attention has been concentrated to a great extent on the Latin American countries with the greatest economic potential and political importance; but its Latin American trade in general has been widespread and very active.

This is not so for Britain and France. However, it is important to point out that the trend for France is on the rise, whereas for Britain it is steadily declining. These two countries seem to have been more selective in establishing their trade links in Latin America and have focused their attention on two types of countries: their ex-colonies (Commonwealth countries in the first case and Départements et Territoires d'Outre Mer — DOM/TOM — in the second), and the upper layer in terms of economic development (namely Argentina, Brazil, Mexico and Venezuela). The case of Argentina, though, is somewhat abnormal, since in 1982 all three countries recorded a strikingly low level of trade with it. This was due not so much to financial difficulties (which Argentina certainly had) as to political problems: the trade embargo imposed on it by the EC member states as a result of the Falklands conflict.

For Britain, Mexico was the largest market in Latin America in 1982, and for France it was Brazil. However, these statements need to be viewed in the context of total global trade: in the British case, Mexico came in 45th position overall, and even though it is of some significance to France as an oil exporter, it still came tenth in the list of France's oil suppliers.

As already noted, ex-colonies take a disproportionate amount of their former masters' trade. France, for instance, consistently exported more in 1980–3 to Guadeloupe and Martinique combined than it did to Brazil. Likewise, during 1981, the UK exported more to the Bahamas alone than to Argentina, Brazil or Venezuela, and imported more from Jamaica during the same year than from Chile, Colombia or Peru.

Despite the relative lack of interest recently shown by Britain and France, there is evidence that both countries are aware of the great potential for future trade expansion in Latin America and are now taking steps to increase their share of trade with the region through identification of potential trade opportunities, marketing and export promotion.[6] But if nothing comes of this, and if Europe slackens its recently renewed attention to the area, Latin America may find other trading alternatives.

The financial crisis which has affected the Third World in general and Latin America in particular has had an interesting effect on the manner in which these countries are conducting their trade relations. Present trends seem to indicate that countertrade (both in commodities and manufactures) is a device which has become increasingly used by developing countries in order to avoid having to resort to payments or credit in hard currencies.[7] In Latin America, General Motors of Brazil has launched a countertrade strategy in the region for the exchange of auto components with Venezuela, Colombia, Ecuador, Uruguay and Chile.[8] Mexico has started barter commerce with Brazil in which, instead of foreign exchange, local currency will be used for items such as auto parts, office equipment and minerals.[9]

Despite a measure of disapproval from governments and international institutions (such as OECD and GATT) of countertrade — on the grounds that it is an impediment to free multilateral commerce — in view of the shortage of foreign exchange in developing countries, barter agreements and countertrade are ways of sidestepping the forced cuts in imports. One estimate is that by 1988 40 per cent of total world trade will be in the form of countertrade, with most of the increase coming from developing countries.[10] It has been argued that countertrade is against the developing countries' interests in the long run.

Countertrade in commodities will eventually be disruptive because it is usually used to get rid of surpluses, thereby stealing market shares from competitors and displacing the exporting country's commercial exports.[11]

Although it is considered inefficient and expensive, governments are beginning to recognize that countertrade is better than no trade at all. Moreover, the banking world has realized that unless it moves into this line of business, it will be left behind by competitors. Already in Great Britain, the European country whose banking and insurance services have been traditionally geared towards the international market, the main clearing banks (Barclays, Midland and Lloyds) are extending their export finance services to meet the demand for putting together countertrade deals.[12] This will not be the first time that trade between Latin America and Europe has taken place via non-conventional agreements.[13]

As already mentioned, European trade with Latin America has acquired some political significance in certain items, namely arms and nuclear technology. In the latter category, a well-known example of important European links with Latin America was the German/ Brazilian nuclear deal, by which Germany was to provide Brazil with eight nuclear power-stations. The contract, signed in 1975 and worth approximately $5 billion, was granted to Kraftwerk Union, and it was the largest export order ever undertaken by the German power-equipment manufacturer. However, the Brazilian financial crisis has caused a freeze in Brazil's nuclear power development, and work on two nuclear stations has been suspended indefinitely. The halting of this programme has been disappointing because at the time the agreement was established it became the epitome of a breakthrough in European/Latin American relations. For Brazil it was concrete proof that there were viable alternatives to US technology transfers; for Germany it was an illustration of increased political independence from the US, which had actively opposed the deal but had had its objections overruled.

The nuclear industry, which at present is going through inauspicious times in industrial countries, does not seem to have better prospects in Latin America. The financial problems that most of the countries in the region are undergoing have led to a reassessment of their energy needs, and they are opting for cheaper alternatives. Nuclear technology is therefore an unlikely area for increased exchanges between Europe and Latin America.

One area, however, in which the European countries have been particularly successful in Latin America is in arms sales. The expanding demand for arms in Latin America, prompted primarily by potential territorial and border disputes, has increasingly been met by Europeans, particularly by France.

Arms trade

A striking feature of Latin America's political development in the last decade or so has been the shift away from the US towards Europe as the main source of military supplies and technology. In the period 1976–80, US arms transfers to Latin America amounted to $725 million, whereas during the same period French arms transfers to the region totalled $1,900 million (Table 2.3). The USA's loss of ground as Latin America's main arms supplier has been the result of two coinciding trends: first, the development of the European military industry and defence thinking; and, second, the change in US relations with Latin America.

In the postwar period, the countries in Western Europe sought to keep a measure of autonomy from the US on defence matters, an aim which had important implications for their overall economic and political independence. The strengthening of their arms industries so as to produce their own armaments efficiently and economically was considered crucial to the retention of this autonomy. The belief that an independent foreign policy should be supported by an autonomous arms industry was particularly strong in France and the UK, above all in France. However, the maintenance of an independent arms production apparatus is a costly exercise, and if a country is to remain internationally competitive in arms production, as well as in research and development, then it must keep its costs down and build in economies of scale. A relatively easy way to achieve this is to increase arms exports, not only to allies and developed countries, but also to the Third World. Latin America proved to be an eager client.

From the perspective of the US, military relations with Latin

Table 2.3 Value of arms transfers, cumulative aggregates 1975–9, 1976–80 and 1978–82, by major supplier and recipient country (current US $ mn)

Supplier / Recipient	1975–9						1976–80						1978–82					
	Total	USSR	USA	France	UK	FRG	Total	USSR	USA	France	UK	FRG	Total	USSR	USA	France	UK	FRG
Latin America	5,000	1,500	725	775	675	440	6,800	2,000	725	1,200	775	450	10,200	3,200	650	1,900	750	400
Argentina	975	–	90	270	60	110	1,100	–	100	340	120	120	1,800	–	100	575	160	120
Barbados	–	–	–	–	–	–	–	–	–	–	–	–	10	–	–	–	10	–
Bolivia	110	–	10	5	–	5	150	–	10	–	–	5	220	–	10	–	–	–
Brazil	725	160	50	400	20	–	800	–	130	30	460	20	675	–	70	–	410	30
Chile	380	–	110	5	40	30	600	–	110	170	50	30	1,100	–	20	500	40	30
Colombia	70	–	20	–	–	40	110	–	30	–	–	–	170	–	50	–	10	20
Costa Rica	–	–	–	–	–	–	–	–	–	–	–	–	5	–	–	–	–	–
Cuba	875	875	–	–	–	–	1,100	1,100	–	–	–	–	2,700	2,600	–	–	–	–
Dominican Rep.	5	–	5	–	–	–	10	–	5	–	–	–	10	–	10	–	–	–
El Salvador	30	–	5	30	–	–	30	–	5	30	–	–	100	–	60	30	–	–
Ecuador	575	–	40	280	70	110	700	–	50	390	70	110	725	–	50	340	70	40
Guatemala	50	–	20	10	–	–	50	–	10	10	–	–	70	–	10	5	–	–
Guyana	10	–	–	–	5	–	10	–	–	–	10	–	10	–	–	–	–	–
Haiti	–	–	–	–	–	–	5	–	–	–	–	–	10	–	–	–	5	–
Honduras	50	–	10	–	–	–	50	–	10	–	–	–	30	–	10	–	10	–
Jamaica	–	–	–	–	–	–	–	–	–	–	–	–	–	–	–	–	–	–
Mexico	70	–	10	–	40	–	70	–	20	10	20	–	270	–	90	20	–	–
Nicaragua	30	–	–	5	–	–	30	–	5	–	–	–	150	–	70	–	–	–
Panama	10	–	–	10	–	–	40	–	40	–	–	–	40	–	30	–	–	–
Paraguay	20	–	–	5	–	–	60	–	5	–	5	–	60	–	–	–	–	5
Peru	1,100	650	100	110	10	40	1,500	900	100	170	10	70	1,200	525	60	260	180	70
Suriname	–	–	–	–	–	–	–	–	–	–	–	–	10	–	–	–	–	–
Trinidad/Tob.	–	–	–	–	–	–	20	–	–	–	–	–	20	–	–	–	–	–
Uruguay	40	–	10	–	–	–	70	–	10	20	120	–	5	–	–	–	–	–
Venezuela	410	–	110	10	60	80	360	–	90	20	30	80	725	–	90	20	5	–

Note: Totals do not necessarily correspond to the sum of all countries included in the table.
Source: US Arms Control and Disarmament Agency, World Military Expenditure and Arms Transfer (Washington, D.C.: ACDA, 1982, 1983, 1984).

America have radically changed since the immediate postwar period, when most Latin American countries were dependent on the US in defence matters through bilateral military agreements and the training of Latin American military personnel in US academies. At present, such military cooperation between Latin American countries and the US is the exception rather than the rule. A number of factors have brought this about. On the US side, Congress's reluctance to prolong the costly tradition of paying for Latin America's arms bills brought these military agreements to an end. At the same time the US pursued a policy of limiting the supply of sophisticated weapons to Latin America. The decreasing US military presence in the region culminated in the Carter administration's policy of imposing arms embargoes on the political regimes which violated human rights.

The Latin American countries' increased drive for independence from the US not only in politico-economic but also in military terms, together with the US policies outlined above, confirmed the belief in Latin America that it was essential to have alternative reliable sources for arms procurement. Some European countries seemed to offer competitive military technology and sophisticated arms, without imposing too many political conditions, and offering special terms of purchase.

The French seemed to find the Latin American arms market very attractive as the US was pulling out, and France offers the best illustration of a country taking advantage of available markets without the imposition of political strings. The French government's justification for this is that by providing an alternative source of military supplies, independent of either of the superpowers, it is giving some countries the possibility of an independent defence policy, and thereby favouring non-aligned tendencies.

The sale of arms is a sensitive issue, not only for commercial reasons, with their implication for important domestic issues, such as industrial development, levels of employment and balance-of-trade benefits (which play a significant role in justifying increased arms exports), but also, of course, for political and strategic reasons. Although several trends in the policies which govern arms sales are discernible, the considerations behind specific deals, their terms of payment and other conditions, are confidential information which it is difficult to obtain. Latin America has not been considered an area which could directly affect the security of a European country, even though the conflict in the South Atlantic may have temporarily altered European perceptions of the region as being relatively conflict-free. Thus, the considerations behind the sales of arms to Latin America have been somewhat different from those governing military exports to regions that are more sensitive for European security, such as the Middle East.

In general the arms trade policies of France, the UK and Germany are directly related to their politico-economic organization and to the structure of their military industry. In France, for example, a large part of the military industry is government-owned and heavily concentrated in a few companies, so that there is a stronger government role in arms development and export policies, a state of affairs which accords with the more centralized French approach. In the UK, whose military industry is scattered among hundreds of mostly private companies, it is difficult for the government to have as large a measure of control as the French government does, and in any case the British government has generally preferred to keep a distance from excessive interference in this type of business.

From a purely political viewpoint, Germany is a special case in defence matters and arms exports, because of its original position in postwar Europe, which resulted in a restrictive policy for arms production. It was not until 1955 that military production in Germany ceased being altogether prohibited. Consequently Germany has kept a low profile in arms exports, through co-production agreements with other countries or through subcontracting. This should be taken into consideration when looking at figures on arms exports from Germany, since these can be misleading. For instance, Germany's arms sales to Latin America appear to have decreased if one compares the aggregates for 1976–80 and 1978–82 (Table 2.3). So it would seem that in this line of exports Germany has lagged considerably behind the UK and France, in contrast with the overall picture for German trade with Latin America. However, in fact, German arms exports have risen steadily during the 1970s and 1980s, although these exports, which have escaped the general guidelines on weapon transfers, have not been made directly from Germany, but from other countries with which Germany has co-production agreements. The export regulations on arms are more restrictive in Germany than they are in France or the UK, but they do not apply to most co-produced weapon systems.[14]

Both the UK and France have increased their arms sales to Latin America, France notably so. In relative terms, however, the role of Britain as a global arms supplier has diminished substantially, not least in Latin America, to which Britain was the second largest weapon exporter after the US during the 1960s. At present France has over-taken both countries by a large margin.

The UK's loss of importance as an arms supplier has been put down to the decolonization process and to Britain's relative loss of influence in world affairs. However, it seems to be more directly related to other considerations, such as restrictions on arms transfers, licensing pro-cedures and, most important, Britain's role in the Atlantic Alliance. Indeed, official attitudes in Europe towards arms exports have been influenced generally by each country's participation in NATO, but there are important differences among the major European arms exporters:

> Britain . . . consults more frequently with NATO's leading military power than with any other European state about political matters, including the implications of its arms exports. This does not mean that Britain usually seeks clearance from Washington, but that on certain occasions it may restrain its impulse to sell equipment . . . France is more flexible in this regard, and freer of self-imposed restraints or allied pressures, as are Italy and West Germany.[15]

The Conservative government in Britain has tried to increase British arms exports. Within the Ministry of Defence, the Defence Sales Organi-zation (DSO) plays an important role in export promotion by serving as a link between companies and foreign governments, advertising British products in magazines, exhibitions, etc., and facilitating the licensing procedures. Export licences are formally granted by the Department of Trade and Industry, although the DSO has an important role in obtaining clearances through the coordination of interministerial committees which consider arms sales. In Britain, export licensing is handled by a department of the MoD, Secretariat 13, whose functions are to control the transfer of sensitive technology and to promote exports. The latter is done by its acting as a link with other ministries involved in reviewing applications: namely, the Treasury, the Foreign and Commonwealth Office and the ECGD.

In France, the licensing procedure goes through the Ministries of Foreign Affairs, Interior and Defence, and, after applications have been reviewed, the licence is granted by the Ministry of Finance.[16] The Délégation Générale pour l'Armement (DGA) is the institution responsible for setting the guidelines for the development of the French military industry, and for establishing a global market network for selling arms.

By the end of the 1960s France had risen to third place in the list of world arms suppliers. Exports of weapons and military technology became 'a critical component of an overall economic strategy'.[17] Although the Middle East and North Africa are by far its largest customers, taking 78.8 per cent of total French arms exports in 1980, Latin America comes third, with 7.0 per cent of the total in the same year. The second place, 7.4 per cent of the total, went to Europe and North America.[18]

France's penetration of the Latin American arms market was convincingly proved by the sale of Mirage fighters to Peru, Brazil, Argentina and Colombia in the late 1960s. Recently it added Bolivia to its list of Mirage customers, and has supplied Argentina with Super Etendard fighters, a variety of Exocet missiles (air-to-ship, ship-to-ship), Lynx and Sagaie armoured cars and AS-332 helicopters.[19] Brazil and Colombia have also received French Exocet ship-to-ship missiles; Peru has bought air-to-ship Exocets. Interestingly, though, the delivery of 29 main battle tanks to Chile, ordered in 1980, was blocked by the Mitterrand government, in accordance with the arms embargo imposed on that country when the Socialist government came to power in France.

There seems to be no evidence that either France or the UK offers official subsidies for arms exports, although in the case of France it has been asserted that to facilitate arms contracts 'advantageous credit arrangements, often at concessionary rates, were made available through such organizations as COFACE'.[20] It is worth mentioning in this connnection that both countries offer military assistance to their ex-colonies. Also, both France and the UK offer credit for arms sales.

In the British case, the credit terms for weapons exports are fixed by the ECGD. Officials state that credit terms for military equipment tend to be more restrictive than civil equipment because of the greater risks involved. Credit terms will vary, but will depend more on the nature of the exports than on the creditworthiness of the country.

In the French case, export credit is also provided, guaranteed by either COFACE or the Banque Française du Commerce Extérieur. The charge for the export credit guarantee is usually 1 per cent of the total value of the contract. However, this charge may be higher or the guarantee refused for contracts which involve special political risks.[21]

As for countertrade, neither France nor Britain accepts barter payments for arms, although there have been exceptions to this, and barter deals between military enterprises and Latin American governments have occasionally occurred. For instance, a report by the Brazilian Air Minister in 1968 stated that the French had agreed to accept partial payment in coffee and raw materials over a period of ten years.

It is virtually impossible to calculate with precision the importance of the Latin American market for European arms exporters, because data are hard to find and may not be accurate. This is especially true for Germany, where the bulk of arms exports take place through co-production agreements with third countries. As for the UK, Latin America has taken an average of between 15 and 30 per cent of its arms exports during the last decade,[22] which means that relatively speaking, although French arms sales to the region are substantially larger, the Latin American market is more important to the UK than to France.

Even in the absence of exact figures, it is safe to assert that weapons exports to out-of-NATO-area countries (including Latin America) have become vital for the maintenance of a competitive and autonomous military industry in Europe. At the same time, Latin American demands for European arms and military technology have been spurred on by the same kind of urge that has led European countries to embark on an autonomous production policy: the desire for a greater margin of independence from the US.

The demand for arms in Latin America rose substantially in the 1970s and is closely related to the existence of numerous areas of potential conflict, territorial or otherwise.[23] These and regional balance-of-power considerations have accounted for a continuous growth in the demand for military hardware, despite rhetorical statements about reducing the levels of arms acquisitions in the region. A good example of disarmament rhetoric in Latin America was the Ayacucho Declaration of 1974, on reducing the arms race in the region, which pledged to make possible 'the limitation of armaments and an end to their acquisition for offensive purposes'. This document, however, has remained a dead letter for most of the signatories (Bolivia, Chile, Colombia, Ecuador, Peru and Venezuela, later joined by Argentina and Panama).

The fact that military exports have become an important line of business for France, mainly for economic but also for political reasons, helps to explain the striking continuity in its arms export policy, both under Giscard d'Estaing and under the Socialist government. Despite pre-election rhetoric about Socialist intentions to reduce military exports, the Mitterrand administration has not only done nothing to reduce them, but has in fact increased them. At present the only countries on which France has imposed an arms embargo are Chile and South Africa. It has been supplying arms to countries like Iran and Libya, and, of great relevance to the topic dealt with here, to Nicaragua. The French decision to sell arms to Nicaragua was taken at the end of 1981 under the assumption that this would help to keep Nicaragua non-aligned. The sale, which included two patrol boats, two Alouette helicopters and ten lorries, though unimportant, was greatly resented by the US; but this opposition did not deter the French from going ahead with the deal and pointing out that these were considered non-offensive weapons.[24] The Germans, however, did bow to US pressure when they cancelled a deal to sell second-hand military vehicles to Nicaragua.[25]

In the UK, no such continuity has existed between Labour and Conservative governments. The current Conservative administration, bent on increasing arms exports, has followed a more pragmatic line than its predecessor, and lifted the arms embargo imposed by the Labour government on Chile. However, a common feature of whichever government is in power in Britain is the great importance granted to fulfilling contracts. Thus, several ships ordered under the Allende government were supplied by Britain after the Chilean coup and under a Labour administration. The justification for this action, which provoked considerable protest, was that those contracts had been signed and Britain would honour them. Since the lifting of the arms embargo, Britain has supplied Chile with two County Class missile destroyers, equipped with MM-38 Exocet missiles, eight Seacat ship-to-air and ship-to-ship missiles and twelve Hunter fighters, and it is negotiating the delivery of twelve Jaguar fighter aircraft, despite domestic and US opposition. It was also contemplating the sale of the 6,200-ton guided missile destroyer HMS Antrim and Sea Eagle air-to-surface missiles.[26] In fact, British pragmatism on arms exports is rather astonishing: after the Falklands conflict Britain urged other governments not to supply weapons to Argentina, and yet 'it honoured contracts of British subcontractors for parts of exactly the same systems, for instance electronics for the French-built Exocet missile and engines for the German-built Meko frigate'.[27]

The future European presence in the Latin American arms market will depend on the level of competitiveness of European military equipment, in terms both of sophistication and of price. This is particularly true of France, since it is the country that has had the most spectacular success in capturing the booming Latin American demand for arms. Competition for arms exports in the future will become increasingly tough, especially now that some Third World countries are becoming important newcomers in the arms trade, notably Israel, Brazil, India and Argentina. It is worth noting that two of these new arms-exporting countries are Latin American, and that in the case of Brazil the arms export business is becoming increasingly important for its economic and military programmes.

Brazil's penetration of the world armaments market is impressive. It is at present selling Tucano and Xingu trainers to the UK, Canada, Belgium, France and Egypt. It also supplies armoured cars (Cascavel) to Algeria and Cyprus. In Latin America it has sold armoured personnel carriers (Urutu) to Colombia and Venezuela (as well as to Saudi Arabia, the United Arab Emirates, Tunisia and Libya) and counterinsurgency Xavante trainers to Ecuador and Argentina. Argentina, too, has been successful in clinching contracts for the supply of the Pucara counterinsurgency trainer to the Central African Republic and El Salvador, and has sold TAM tanks (the end-product of a collaborative production scheme with West Germany) to Peru and Iran.

The European countries' loss of ground in Latin America's trade became exacerbated by the drastic cuts in imports most countries in the region implemented as a result of their acute financial problems. However, the European countries have realized that despite the present austerity measures taken by most governments in Latin America, the region can still be a promising market for certain of their exports, not least arms.

In view of increasing international trade competition, the European countries have sought ways of making their exports to Latin America more competitive, by means of attractive credit facilities or by adding a measure of aid funds to their export contracts. In addition to these financing facilities, which may run into problems given the level of Latin America's external debt difficulties, some European countries have launched export-promotion campaigns. The general strategy has been to concentrate on the products in which the exporting country has a comparative advantage, as in the case of Britain, and not to discriminate against standard consumer products in order to favour only capital goods or large-scale contracts, as in the case of France. Another approach has been to concentrate on those countries with a greater economic potential, instead of spreading exports thinly throughout the region, although in the case of the two colonial powers in Latin America, Britain and France, trade with their dependencies far exceeds that with other, more important countries.

3 Development assistance

It has not been until relatively recently that development assistance acquired a special significance for governments and became an issue in public opinion. This was a result of the growing realization by the less developed countries (LDCs) that in an increasingly interdependent world the industrialized countries had to share the responsibility for their development. The LDCs were particularly active in the late 1970s in applying pressure for the establishment of a New International Economic Order. The Latin American countries participated wholeheartedly in this and took a special interest in what became known as the North/South dialogue. How the Latin American countries have been regarded by Europe within the context of development assistance and whether they have been successful in achieving a large share of Europe's external aid funds are the questions this chapter seeks to answer.

Overview

Aid flows from developed to developing countries are made up of the bilateral (or multilateral) transfer of financial assets (official or private), other kinds of assistance in the form of donations of goods and services (such as food or military aid), project appraisal, and educational and cultural cooperation.

The OECD's Development Assistance Committee (DAC) breaks up the total official flows from its member countries into official development assistance (oda), which comprises concessional flows for development, and other official flows (oof), which may consist of loans for development which do not qualify as oda, grants by the export credit agencies for interest stabilization, official export credits and equity investments. The total official flows consist of the sum of oda and oof.[1]

In general, the members of the DAC, which include the three countries under review, have one agency or ministry that bears the main responsibility for administering aid, although there are a score of other official institutions that are likely to intervene in the political and economic questions involved in assistance programmes. These institutions will vary according to the organization of the country in question, but will usually comprise the Treasury and the Ministries of Trade, Industry and Foreign Affairs, as well as the components of the export credit financing systems of each country.

From the mid-1970s, attacking absolute poverty and satisfying basic needs has been a matter of world concern and the main rationale behind the aid strategies of industrialized countries towards developing areas. Therefore, the aid policies of countries such as France, Germany and the UK do not make Latin America a priority for aid, in view of the relatively high income levels of most Latin American countries. They have tended instead to concentrate on the poorest areas, such as Africa and Asia, or have given priority to those areas with which they have had closest ties: France and the UK to their ex-colonies, Germany to Turkey.

The United Nations General Assembly, as part of the Development Strategy for the Second UN Development Decade, called upon the developed countries to meet a target for the flows classified as oda of at least 0.7 per cent of the GNP of the donor country. This target was generally accepted, though the date for its achievement was not set. In fact, although these three countries are among the five largest contributors of the DAC, none of them has reached the 0.7 per cent target.[2]

Since the Latin American states are not considered to be the most needy (with the exception of Haiti and Honduras), the aid policies of France, the UK and West Germany towards Latin America can acquire more political or commercial undertones than aid devoted to other areas. Official aid for development to Latin America can have important implications for the kind of political and economic relations that Europe wants to pursue in the area. These considerations may in fact outweigh the development purposes which are generally advanced for the granting of economic aid.

The best example of aid policies that allegedly benefit the recipient as well as the donor country's exports are the 'mixed credits', i.e., a combination of normal export credits and aid funds. This practice, started by France, soon caught on with other countries. It was regarded by France as falling within the scope of development assistance and indeed, for non-francophone countries, it is the only form of aid that France provides. Although the official view is that the main purpose of mixed credits is to channel aid to the less well-off, and that their effect on French exports is secondary, France has used them to get ahead in the export race by adding the aid component to match the favourable terms of other countries. However, aid funds began to be more commonly added to export credit packages by other countries as well, with the result that terms for prospective importers became increasingly attractive. At the same time, the addition of aid funds to export credits brought an extra dimension to the already tight competition among industrial nations in offering the best credit terms and thereby clinching more export contracts.

Recently, however, there have been claims that mixed credits have an adverse effect both on developing countries and on the exporting developed countries, which compete to better each other's terms. Growing concern about the way this 'associated financing' distorted trade led the members of the DAC to adopt in June 1983 the 'Guiding principles for the use of aid in association with export credits and other market funds', in order to regulate the amount of aid each export credit could entail.[3]

There are a number of differences in French, British and German attitudes towards mixed credits. It is not surprising that it was France, a country with a more centralized approach to economic and industrial matters, which initiated the practice. Britain followed suit, and bilateral aid through mixed credits has become a basic feature of its overseas development aid policies. The standpoint of Germany on the issue is rather more negative than that of Britain or France. Germany's preference for a laissez-faire approach, together with its industrial competitiveness, means there is less call for an interventionist policy. However, the pressures to reduce balance-of-payments costs as well as to increase levels of employment have led Germany to back away from its liberal practices and to allocate a considerable portion of mixed credits to its aid.

Another aspect of aid which links it to export promotion is its 'tying status'. This refers to how much of a loan or grant may be used for the purchase of goods and services in the recipient country or in third countries, as opposed to the donor country. In the case of Britain, bilateral technical cooperation is almost wholly tied to UK procurement. In the case of Germany, there has also been an increasing trend to tie financial aid to national procurement, although in 1981, 'about 60 per cent of [united] bilateral financial and technical assistance led to national procurement'.[4] An interesting comparison of the attitudes of these countries to tied aid is given by Table 3.1, which shows their 'delinking coefficients', namely the ratios of non-tied development aid to total aid (expressed as a percentage).

Table 3.1 Delinking coefficients: France, FRG, UK, 1979

	France	FRG	UK
Total development aid (US $ mn)	4,112	4,013	2,256
United aid (US $ mn)	1,696	3,057	897
Delinking coefficient	41%	76%	40%

Source: B. Nezeys, *Les Relations économiques extérieures de la France* (Paris: Economica, 1982), p. 135.

The policy of tying aid to the purchase of goods and services from the donor countries has received criticism from what can be considered to be the two opposite poles of the political spectrum. The progressives claim that tied aid may be a means of increasing the donor country's trade, with consequent beneficial effects on its balance of payments, but that it does little in the majority of cases to satisfy the real needs of the developing countries, and does not serve the purpose of helping their economic development. From a purely pragmatic point of view, tied aid is criticized on the grounds that, like other forms of subsidization, it distorts market forces and 'pushes the world away from a rational organization of production based on comparative advantage'.[5]

Germany

With no colonial commitments Germany has been relatively free to pursue aid policies in line with national priorities, including political, economic and humanitarian aims. The geographical distribution of German oda, as stated in a number of policy documents since 1975, is assigned to give priority to the least developed countries (LLDCs). The areas on which German aid policy seeks to concentrate are rural development and food production.[6]

German policy on oda has shown a remarkable continuity, from the issuing of the Development Policy Concept, first adopted by the German Federal government in 1971, to the Kohl administration guidelines on aid. The Development Policy Concept has been expanded gradually to include statements concerning a European development policy, the protection of the environment and the use of mineral resources, but the main emphasis has been kept on measures designed to combat absolute poverty (basic needs concept).

At present the document setting the guidelines on aid policy is the fifth report on development policy, submitted to the Bundestag in early 1983. Although apparently no major change has taken place in the general principles on aid policies, emphasis is now being put on cooperation with the private sector and the 'intensification of the policy dialogue with aid recipients'.[7] This means that recipient countries are being expected to react to German oda by granting favourable conditions for German investment, 'a reduced state role in the economy, price flexibility, a "realistic" exchange rate and export promotion benefits'.[8] And, though no major change has taken place, there is a more explicit will on the German side to obtain some tangible results from oda which will benefit German industry and the economy as a whole.

Before Chancellor Kohl took power, German policy towards Latin America was to diminish the flows of aid to the region, given the relatively high GNP per capita of most of the countries therein. Of course some exceptions were made for countries like Bolivia, Ecuador, Haiti, Jamaica and Honduras, but richer countries, such as Peru and Brazil, have been recipients of not negligible amounts of German aid. In the period 1980-1 they received 1.4 and 1.9 per cent of total

German oda respectively. No German aid is earmarked for Communist countries, so Cuba does not figure among the recipients of German aid.

There are two other factors — apart from income levels — that help explain why Latin America has received the smallest share of German bilateral assistance.[9] First, Latin America has been regarded traditionally as being the exclusive sphere of influence of the US. Thus German development policy in Latin America has relied more on non-governmental organizations than on official institutions. In the former category, the Churches, trade unions and other social groups and political associations have played an important role. The political foundations associated with parties represented in the Bundestag have been particularly active in offering technical assistance and funds, as well as political advice, to like-minded parties in Latin America. This last point will be discussed in more detail in the second part of this essay. The second reason for the relative lack of German official interest in Latin America as an area for oda is that the region has been regarded as more suitable for private businesss cooperation rather than as a needy recipient of public aid.

Over the past two decades German aid to Latin America has amounted to approximately $3 billion, of which the main benificiaries have been Brazil ($700 million), Peru ($500 million), and Chile ($300 million) until 1973, when German aid stopped. The priority countries in the region for the Kohl administration are now those of the Caribbean and Central America, in particular the Dominican Republic, Jamaica, Haiti, Costa Rica, El Salvador and Honduras.[10]

In the specific cases in which German bilateral aid is channelled to Latin American countries, the areas to which emphasis is given are in line with its general development cooperation policy, namely health, rural development, and food production. The major recipient of German aid in 1983 was Peru, where aid funds went to rural agricultural programmes, health care and fishing and mining industries. In the Dominican Republic, aid was concentrated on improving port facilities and electricity supplies. In Jamaica, the bulk of the aid went to the development of the sugar industry.

Political factors have become increasingly important in determining the allocation of German aid to Latin America. A good example of the

44

politicization of aid is the recent German attitude towards Central American countries. Aid to El Salvador, which had remained at a standstill for five years while the SPD/FDP coalition was in power, was resumed under the Kohl administration when it was considered that the democratization process had been advanced in that country. Consequently a new DM 51 million aid package was finalized during President José Napoleón Durate's visit to Bonn in the summer of 1984.[11] By contrast, aid to Nicaragua, which was not negligible during the days of Schmidt, has been frozen under Kohl on the grounds that no aid will be forthcoming until real political pluralism is permitted by the Sandinistas. This attitude is evidence of some of the new views on foreign aid introduced by the Kohl administration to bring Germany more in line with the US, not least on flows of aid to Latin America. Perhaps on account of the political tension in the region, particularly in Central America, with its implications for the East/West confrontation, and because of what has been described as Kohl's rediscovery of America, Germany has decided to increase its economic aid programme to Latin America, from 9 per cent of the total German aid budget to 10.4 per cent.[12]

According to the German government, economic aid is granted according to need, through grants, long-term technical assistance and also mixed credits. As was seen above, mixed credits are becoming an increasingly large component of German aid, although there is no unified attitude towards them within the German government. Increasing the number of mixed credits is regarded with disfavour in the Economics Ministry, an attitude not untypical of the general hard line towards North/South issues which is usually taken by ministries of economics or finance, in contrast with the softer line found in the ministries of foreign affairs or economic cooperation. Not surprisingly, a more positive attitude towards mixed credits in Germany is found in the Ministry of Foreign Affairs, in which mixed credits are considered to be an effective method of helping the development process in Third World countries, especially the NICs, which still cannot compete on a par with industrialized countries.[13]

Investment plays a very important part in Germany's policies on economic and development cooperation. The emphasis given to investment in developing countries is consistent with the German belief in the role of the private sector as the engine of economic growth, and with its approach to Latin America as an area that is suitable for private cooperation. In line with these beliefs, in 1962 the German government set up a non-profit-making institution, the Deutsche Entwicklungsgesellschaft (DEG), or German Development Company, which will be examined more closely in the section on investment.

Germany, like Britain and France, prefers bilateral to multilateral aid. The reason behind this preference is that bilateral aid can be more easily controlled and can better serve the purpose of the donor. In the period 1980–1 German multilateral aid amounted to just 27.5 per cent of total aid for development.

The United Kingdom

The priority areas for British aid are the poorest countries worldwide, and, as in the case of France, particularly close attention is paid to former dependencies. For this reason Latin American countries are far from being central to British oda. The Commonwealth as a whole and individual countries within it have received on average during the last decade about two thirds of British oda. In the period 1980–1 British oda was mainly concentrated in five countries, which together received 28.5 per cent of the total. These countries were India, Bangladesh, Tanzania, Sri Lanka and Kenya.

In 1979 the newly elected Conservative government turned the Overseas Development Ministry (ODM) into the Overseas Development Administration (ODA), with responsibility for administering British oda. The ODA became closely integrated with the FCO (although administratively the two staffs remain separate).[14] The department in charge of aid has been in a weak political position since it was first created (in 1964). Until very recently, aid was a non-issue in British politics: it had few supporters in Whitehall and had not attracted the attention of the general public. It is therefore not surprising that there was little public debate when aid funds were greatly affected by the general policy of pruning public expenditure. At the same time, the geographical distribution of aid became more heavily influenced by political and commercial objectives. Thus, in principle, bilateral financial assistance from the UK is now tied to the procurement of British goods and services, and this is particularly so in the case of Latin America. This policy is openly acknowledged and has been justified by the present Overseas Development Minister, Timothy Raison: 'We owe it to the poor not to wash our hands of their misery, but we are also in the business of looking after Britain's political and trading interests, and interests in promoting stability in countries which could slide into chaos with dangerous and unpredictable effects on the security of all of us.'[15]

As in the case of Germany, British policy favours bilateral rather than multilateral aid, a fact that was stressed by Mr Raison when he stated that bilateral aid 'has obvious political and commercial advantages over multilateral aid.'[16] However, although bilateral aid is considered an essential instrument of British commercial and diplomatic policy, Britain's multilateral aid budget has shown a remarkable growth, from less than 10 per cent of total aid in the 1960s to 40.7 per cent in 1979–80. It fell slightly to 34.6 per cent in 1980–1, but rose again to 41 per cent in 1983.[17]

British bilateral financial aid is divided into project and non-project aid. The latter is provided for such purposes as programme aid, budgetary aid, debt cancellation or refinancing, food and fertilizer aid, and disaster relief. The former is used for the establishment or expansion of production and infrastructure facilities: its funds are provided by the Commonwealth Development Cooperation (CDC), through investments overseas, and by the ODA. Funds from the ODA for project aid may come from its regular country programmes or from the Aid and Trade Provision (ATP). ATP is used mainly to enable British firms to match offers of mixed credits made by other countries, and it is funded from the ODA's allocations.

The importance of matching the terms of mixed credits offered by other countries and thereby helping British exporters is illustrated by the fact that although Latin America ranks very low as a recipient of British aid, Mexico came fourth in the 1982 list of main bilateral recipients of British oda. In that year Mexico received a total of £34 million in aid (coming after India with £54 million, Sudan with £39 million and Kenya with £37 million). Of the £34 million Mexico received as aid, 97 per cent was in the form of ATP, i.e., it helped finance British exports to Mexico, mainly for the steelworks built by

Davy Construction for the Mexican steel mill, Sicartsa.[18] This case contradicts, at least as far as Latin America is concerned, the basic guidelines for British aid policy: that priority should be given to the poorest countries.

In fact a look at British figures on aid to Latin America would point to other criteria — difficult to discern, though commercial considerations may be high among them — than national poverty for granting official aid. If aid to the poorest countries were actually the guideline, then Haiti, the only Latin American country to rank among the poorest fifty in the world, should come high in the list of aid recipients and receive proportionately the largest share. But Haiti in 1982 received only £1,000 in aid (an amount that rose to £19,000 in 1983), placing it way down the list of Latin American recipients of British oda, and even below Venezuela, the Latin American country with the largest GNP per capita. So, apart from very general statements on the policy governing the granting of aid, which are in fact contradicted by the practice, it would seem that Britain does not have a clear-cut aid policy towards the area.

France

Like Britain, France concentrates a large part of its oda on its ex-colonies. In the period 1980–1 French aid to the DOM/TOM amounted to 38.7 per cent of total (including multilateral) oda. And it should be remembered that the DOM are an integral part of French territory.

The change of government in France also introduced a new policy approach to aid and the Third World. In the Socialist electoral platform, overseas development aid was high on the agenda and was regarded as an important element in the global political programme. This was justified in political as well as strategic terms by the Socialist conviction that international power confrontations would very likely take place in the Third World.[19] The Common Programme 1972–7, endorsed by the French Socialist and Communist Parties, emphasized the adoption of a policy of international cooperation based on genuine independence and of non-intervention in the economic and political affairs of the developing countries. Both parties committed themselves to the support of official aid over and above private-sector initiatives, including commercial interests.

The strongest criticism of the aid policy of the Giscard d'Estaing government came from the Socialist Party, which stressed that during his administration most French aid was tied to buying French equipment, thereby benefiting French companies and using aid funds to subsidize French exports at the expense of the recipient countries. On taking power, the Socialist government made an evaluation of the aid programmes of the preceding administration with a view to reforming them. Among its findings it concluded that not only had French Treasury loans been an excessive financial burden to France, but they had 'financed a frenzied policy of exports rather than a policy of internal development of the recipient'.[20] But the Socialist aim of radically altering France's traditional aid policies is likely to run into two main obstacles: first, there is no clearly outlined development policy for non-francophone countries; and, second, any policy will be fragmented among several ministries and institutions.[21] However, although the general policy framework may be lacking, the French priority areas for assistance have been singled out: in order of importance, the whole of Africa (not just francophone), the LLDCs and multilateral aid. This last category may be significant, since France's contribution to multilateral oda is small indeed. As a proportion of the respective budgets, the French share of 16.3 per cent of total oda compared very unfavourably with Germany's 27.5 per cent and Britain's 34.6 per cent in the period 1980-1. In the league table of recipients of French foreign aid, the Latin American countries hardly rank at all: Brazil, in the years 1980-1, received 1.6 per cent of total French oda in a list headed by Réunion, with 13.9 per cent.

Of the eight industrialized countries' leaders who met their counterparts from fourteen developing countries at the Cancún Summit Conference on International Cooperation and Development in Mexico in 1981 (the first of its kind), it was President Mitterrand who seemed to attach most importance to the continuation of the North/South dialogue as a means of working towards the New International Economic Order. However, the pronouncements of French policymakers on increasing aid to less developed areas repeatedly point to the lack of French resources as an impediment to greater amounts of aid or its wider distribution to areas other than Africa. Consequently it has

49

been pointed out that French aid to Central America cannot be forth-coming, except in the form of diplomatic aid. It is therefore stressed that the aid granted to Nicaragua in the form of food and light weapon transfers can only have a symbolic significance; France could not possibly go further without compromising its position in Africa.[22]

Generally speaking, Latin America has not been a leading recipient of European aid, and this has been due to two basic factors: first, because of its relatively high income levels when compared with other areas of the Third World, it does not qualify for aid as such (although on this count some countries within the region — Haiti and Honduras — deserve more attention from DAC countries than hitherto); and second, aid funds of countries such as France and the UK have often tended to be channelled to former colonies. There is, however, one area in which Latin America has not been unimportant for European aid: as a recipient of mixed credits, whose main result has been to help European exports rather than contribute to development assistance.

4 Investment

Overview

For Latin America, as well as for the rest of the developing world, a major source of finance, together with development assistance and private bank lending, has been foreign direct investment (FDI). Outward direct investment has been regarded by the industrialized countries as an effective instrument of development cooperation. However, the recipient countries have had mixed feelings about FDI, since it can introduce a measure of foreign control in the management of dynamic parts of the host country's economic activity. The advantages and disadvantages of FDI, for both host and home countries, have been the subject of continuous debate.

In Latin America, the general attitude towards FDI has gone through a cycle of positive and negative phases, alternatively highlighting the costs and the benefits. During the 1950s and 1960s, FDI was regarded as an integral part of the import substitution model, and its beneficial features for economic development were at the forefront. Later on, there was an overreaction against FDI, in the late 1960s and early 1970s. Especially after the formation of the Andean Pact in 1969 as a regional subgrouping, a more restrictive attitude emerged in most of Latin America, and a wave of nationalizations which took place in Peru, Chile and Bolivia marked a low ebb for FDI in the region. At present, however, the cycle has changed yet again and, partly as a result of the economic constraints imposed by debt problems, there has been a more balanced reassessment of FDI on the part of recipient countries, which seem to have overcome their resistance to it in principle.

Within the net flow of all financial resources from developed to developing countries, the share of direct investment has followed a decreasing trend in recent years: from 20.2 per cent during the 1960s to 18.5 per cent during the 1970s.[1] On average FDI flows from DAC countries grew during the 1970s at a rate of roughly 15 per cent annually in nominal terms and 5 per cent in real terms, but FDI grew considerably more slowly than some other types of non-concessional resources. By contrast, total domestic investment in developing countries increased by an average of around 6 per cent annually during the same period, and there was a larger proportion of domestic than foreign investment.

The decrease in FDI in developing countries coincided with a considerable increase in international private bank lending (especially in the form of syndicated Eurocurrency credits). The choice between private credits and FDI was influenced by the 'foreign control' concern of the recipient, the drawback of FDI is that the foreign investor will try to take as much of his profits abroad as possible; the charge for the other hand it could be argued that investment not only provides a flow of capital, but at the same time a transfer of technology, managerial expertise and general know-how. From the point of view of the recipient, the drawback of the FDI is that the foreign investor will try to take as much of his profits abroad as possible; the charge for a loan, however, will depend on the loan's performance, which is out of the control of the recipients. (It is worth noting at this point that although a large share of loans were used in Latin America to provide balance-of-payments support, some lending did relate directly to investment projects, which would not have been possible without external financing.)

Despite the relative decrease in FDI in developing countries, it is still regarded as a major source of finance, especially for Latin America. Moreover, FDI will acquire a growing importance for debtor countries, because there is a lack of domestic financial resources for investment: most public (and private) funds are going at present into debt-servicing.

Foreign investment from developed to developing countries has tended to concentrate on middle- and high-income countries: for example, Argentina, Brazil, Mexico, Venezuela and Peru held more than 50 per cent of the regional FDI stocks during the period 1971-8.[2] In fact, in 1978, Brazil and Mexico together held 38 per cent of all

FDI stocks from DAC countries to Latin America and 20 per cent of the overall total for developing countries.

The US is still the main supplier of FDI flows to developing countries (almost 60 per cent of the total in 1979); other major sources are the UK, Japan and West Germany. Together these four countries provided 82 per cent of all DAC investment in 1979. In that year about one third of all DAC FDI went to developing countries, and almost two thirds of that went to Latin America. Within this overall pattern of US dominance as the largest supplier of investment, it is only natural that it should continue to be the major supplier of FDI to Latin America. However, in the past decade, the West European countries, notably Germany and the UK, have substantially increased their share of FDI to the region.

The pattern of UK investment in Latin America is rather interesting. From having been by far the most important foreign investor in the region during the nineteenth century, it had been overtaken by the US by the turn of this century. In 1930, 35 per cent of British direct investments overseas were in Latin America, but by 1971 these had declined to 7 per cent and in 1974 to 4.5 per cent of the total. In the period 1978–81, however, Latin America's participation in total British outward investment increased one percentage point from 5 to 6. Although there is no direct evidence to explain this sudden reversal of an otherwise declining investment trend, it may have had something to do with the lifting of exchange controls in 1979.

Germany's importance as a major source of foreign investment for developing countries has gradually been increasing, and during the 1970s it became almost as important as the UK and Japan as a source of direct investment in the Third World. Of the European investors, Germany is the country which has concentrated its attention most heavily on Latin America. By the end of 1979 the accumulated book value of these investments was approximately DM 8 billion, which amounted to 50 per cent of German investments in developing countries and 13 per cent of total investments abroad. German investments in Brazil now make up 60 per cent of the country's total in developing countries, and Brazil, Argentina and Mexico hold 80 per cent of German investments in Latin America.

Although during the 1960s France was an important investor in developing areas, its share appears to have declined in the 1970s, particularly during the second half of the decade. Its investments within the French franc area are free from restrictions, but direct investment transfers, including loans constituting a direct investment, require prior declaration to the Minister of Economy, Finance and the Budget. Unless specifically exempted, 75 per cent of investment abroad has to be financed from foreign sources (not unlike the situation in the UK prior to the lifting of exchange controls). However, despite these apparent disincentives for investing in regions other than the French franc area, investment by France in Latin America exceeded that in Africa during the period 1979–81 (see Table 4.1).

Table 4.1 Distribution of geographically allocated direct investment flows (net) from major source countries, 1979–81 (%)*

	Europe	Latin America	Africa	Asia	Total
France	33 (34)	39 (6)	23 (16)	5 (2)	100
FRG	21 (18)	59 (7)	5 (3)	15 (4)	100
Japan	1 (4)	29 (11)	9 (16)	61 (49)	100
UK†	10 (13)	36 (7)	30 (25)	24 (9)	100
US	5 (31)	69 (69)	9 (40)	17 (36)	100

*Figures in parentheses denote the home countries' share in the total FDI of the continent from the five source countries (including official support for private investment by the Japanese government).
†Excluding investments in the oil industry.
Source: OECD, *Investing in Developing Countries* (5th rev. edn, Paris, 1983), p 18.

Investment policies in Europe and Latin America

Investment strategies in general and the outflow of direct investment depend on a number of economic and non-economic factors in home and host countries as well as on the international economy. The policies of home countries as originators of FDI vary according to their objectives: in general, industrialized countries encourage FDI, since it can be considered an effective instrument of development cooperation and because it can benefit the home country's economy. To the extent that it will improve export and import opportunities and increase the competitiveness of its national enterprises, a government is likely to support foreign investment and aim at securing the protection of direct investment abroad and guaranteeing the full benefits of the foreign operations of its enterprises.

The incentives provided by home countries are numerous. To begin with, they ensure that the same treatment is granted to capital invested overseas and profits derived from it as is given to inward investment and its income. Governments also offer investment guarantee schemes to cover political as opposed to commercial risks, although the actual amount involved is insignificant: on average only 9–10 per cent of FDI stock originating in DAC countries is under insurance cover (in the case of the countries under study, 4 per cent for France, 10 per cent for Germany and 20 per cent for the UK). Insurance schemes are relatively recent and do not include investments prior to their establishment. Furthermore, it has been stated that, to avoid excessive bureaucratic procedures, big firms, especially well-established transnational corporations (TNCs), prefer self-insurance. The agencies which provide investment guarantees are: in France, COFACE and the Banque Française du Commerce Extérieur (BFCE); in Germany, Treuarbeit; and in the UK, the ECGD. In the case of Germany, the government has followed the practice of applying for investment guarantee agreements with Latin American governments in order to create incentives for private investors by increasing their confidence in the safety of their investments.

Another type of instrument for encouraging FDI from the home country is fiscal measures, such as 'tax-deferral', in which the investor is allowed to deduct the foreign taxes paid on investment income from his national income tax. These deferrals can arise from domestic legislation or from bilateral treaties with host countries in order to avoid double taxation. Other fiscal measures include the partial financing of, or reimbursement for, pre-investment feasibility studies. Germany has recently expanded this type of programme, as have the US and Japan. Finally, governments sometimes offer official support to private investors in developing countries by granting 'second-rank loans' for the establishment of small and medium-sized enterprises.

France and Germany have introduced this type of loan.

Official support for private investment in its most institutionalized form is that provided by the public development finance corporations of some industrialized countries. In the French case, the most important of these official institutions is the Caisse Centrale de Coopération Economique (CCCE), whose main function is to administer official aid, in the form of loans at preferential interest rates, to ex-colonies and African countries. The CCCE, however, plays an important role in private financing as well, by providing support in the form of medium-term rediscount credits, long-term loans and, to a very small extent, equity participation. The CCCE does not deal with Latin America except for some small loans to Haiti. Another French financial institution is the Union pour le Financement et l'Expansion du Commerce International (UFINEX), which provides loans for financing outward investment, although its criterion for doing so is that it will only participate in investments that will generate, within a five-year period, a volume of French exports three or four times greater than the initial investment. The proportion of the loans provided by UFINEX varies between 50 and 60 per cent of the investment. But it is more than an investment scheme, performing rather as an export promotion instrument. Other institutions with similar functions are the Fonds d'Aide et de Coopération (FAC) and the Développement Industriel à l'Etranger.

The German government's agency for investment in developing countries is the DEG (Deutsche Entwicklungsgesellschaft). It provides official equity capital for German private investment in small and medium-size enterprises in developing countries. The German government provides a minority share and the German private investor and local capital provide the majority. The DEG does not normally provide more than half of total finance. The German government's encouragement of this type of official participation has two objectives in mind: to help the development of joint ventures in developing countries; and to obtain more favourable conditions for its enterprises as a result of their being regarded as 'neutral' (because of the local capital) rather than purely German. The functions of the DEG, as well as its *raison d'être*, were heavily influenced by the International Finance Corporation (IFC) of the World Bank, and by the British Commonwealth

Development Corporation. In 1980, the DEG distribution of funds was as follows: Asia, 58 per cent of total commitments; Africa, 22 per cent; Latin America, 11 per cent; and Europe 9 per cent.[3] The low percentage of DEG activities in Latin America may be a reflection of the reluctance of small and medium-size firms to become established in the area because it has been traditionally regarded as the recipient of investment from big corporations.

The UK's Commonwealth Development Corporation (CDC) was established in 1948 to help the economic development of the British dependent territories. Although originally its activities were to be aimed exclusively at the Commonwealth countries, ministerial approval has since been obtained for activities that cover other developing countries. At present, in Latin America, the CDC's activities are aimed at Costa Rica, Ecuador and Honduras. There are no policy criteria for this expansion into non-Commonwealth, Latin American countries. Low income could provide a justification for the inclusion of Ecuador and Honduras, but the CDC's presence in Costa Rica, classified as an upper/middle-income country (far better off in GNP per capita terms than Guatemala, El Salvador or Nicaragua), cannot be justified on grounds of poverty. It is interesting to point out, though, that the CDC's investments, in contrast with UFINEX, for instance, are not tied to UK procurement.

Naturally, the policies of the host countries towards FDI will have an important impact on any investment decisions by foreign firms. It has been stressed more than once in the OECD Development Cooperation Review that 'the decisive and irreplaceable prerequisite which host countries can provide is an attractive "investment climate"'. What is meant by that is that host countries should offer the necessary, and even ideal, conditions for foreign investment: namely, a reduction in the costs of production for the foreign investors by means of tax holidays and direct subsidies.[4] Perhaps other incentives foreign investors should look for when investing in developing countries are the more traditional ones, such as the host country's resources, cheaper labour and wider margins of profit, growth prospects and political stability.

Host countries can have very effective tools for controlling FDI, the purpose of which is to adapt FDI to national economic objectives and development plans, and to achieve a trade-off between the costs and the benefits of external capital to individual sectors. Some of the restrictions imposed by host countries are: barring FDI in sensitive sectors (national defence, public utilities, transportation and telecommunications, mass media, banking and insurance, etc.); setting an upper limit on the share of foreign equity participation, and on the amount of capital and profits that can be repatriated; setting a lower limit on the share of FDI-generated products that can be exported; insisting on local participation in the management of foreign enterprises; price controls; and that ultimate instrument of FDI control, nationalization. All these forms of regulation have been exercised in one form or another by the Latin American countries, which at various moments in their history have resorted to variable doses of economic nationalism.

In addition, the Latin American states have traditionally been opposed to international arbitration in investment disputes, claiming that it is a derogation of their sovereignty. Consequently, the Calvo doctrine, which allows foreigners to refuse the protection of their home governments and, for legal purposes, to be considered as nationals of the country they have invested in, has been adopted by the majority of the countries in the region. In accordance with this doctrine, they have consistently resisted accession to the convention of the International Court for the Settlement of Investment Disputes (ICSID).

Perhaps the anxiety of host countries about losing control of their economic decision-making has led to the establishment, since the early 1970s, of new forms of investment which in general tend to reduce the extent of foreign control. These new forms of investment include joint ventures, minority participations, production-sharing and sub-contracting agreements, licensing and marketing contracts, turnkey projects, and buy-back, co-financing and trilateral financing arrangements.[5] They constitute a significant shift in the nature of foreign participation since, traditionally, the investor's purpose was to have an effective voice in the management of the enterprise.

However, as has been mentioned above, the climate for foreign investment in Latin America has gradually become more favourable of late. This has been more the result of the need for funds than of the countries' being converted to the case for foreign investment. The lack of domestic capital and the tight market for new foreign borrowing have forced the Latin American countries to ease the conditions for new FDI and to lift some of the restrictions previously imposed on it.

The Andean Pact countries had adopted a common set of rules for FDI: 51 per cent of the shares had to be in the hands of nationals; there had to be a phase-out formula, i.e., the gradual conversion of foreign enterprises into joint ventures; Decision 24 limited the remittances of profits; foreign firms had to be in a less favourable position than national ones with regard to credit facilities and intraregional trade, and so on. In fact, some of the conditions for FDI were so stringent that concessions were made even before the financial crisis. For example, Decision 103 was introduced, which increased the allowance for the transfer of capital and earnings from 14 to 20 per cent. At present, and less formally, the Andean Pact countries have turned a blind eye to regulations on foreign investment. Venezuela is providing investors with better conditions; they are now allowed on the boards of national companies and are able to buy real estate. Ecuador, where foreign firms are eager to get a larger share in the exploitation of newly found oil deposits, has offered the foreign companies all the guarantees they have demanded, some of which are in violation of Decision 24.[6] Mexico was traditionally a country in which foreign investment laws were very strict and did not permit majority foreign participation, but it is allowed now − in industries that fall within a list of 34 categories (including electrical and non-electrical machinery and equipment, chemical industry, hotels, etc.). The conditions now are that new investments should generate foreign exchange, contribute to scientific and technological development, increase employment, substitute imports, and contribute to the economic decentralization of Mexico.

Another interesting development in Mexico's new attitude to FDI is that it is allowing greater foreign participation in state-controlled enterprises, which until recently was carefully restricted. France is taking advantage of Mexico's new investment climate. Renault is extending its 40 per cent interest there by acquiring the Mexican government's 60 per cent share in Renault de Mexico and Mexican Automotive Vehicles. It plans to expand production of heavy and light trucks, and to boost car sales. The test case for Mexico's new investment climate is the fate of IBM's plans to establish a major wholly owned subsidiary for the production and export of personal computers. The Foreign Investment Commission has rejected the application because of IBM's refusal to accept the inclusion of additional clauses in the contract in line with Mexico's overall development strategy. However, the rejection may not be final and further talks on this may take place at a future stage.

Patterns of European investment in Latin America

As was stressed above, it is the medium- and high-income countries in which the bulk of FDI seems to be concentrated. The Latin American NICs (Brazil, Mexico and — to a lesser extent — Argentina) have been the most important recipients of FDI in the last decade. This pattern is followed by Britain, France and Germany: not surprisingly, their investment in Latin America has also been centred on the most dynamic economies of the region.

Investment is also concentrated in certain sectors; in others, almost no FDI can be found. This pattern has changed through time. Before World War II, most foreign investments in the region were located in public utilities, and in the agricultural and extractive sectors. In the postwar period, investments in utilities substantially declined. With the exception of oil, the bulk of foreign investment moved massively to the more dynamic sectors of the economy, like manufacturing, where foreign control became relatively high. This was in line with the region's import-substitution drive, a strategy in which FDI played an integral part. Today, within the manufacturing sector, certain industries tend to be more under foreign control than others: in Mexico and Peru, 67 per cent of the chemical industries is foreign-owned; in Brazil, 99 per cent of the motor assembly industry; and in Argentina, 82 per cent of nonelectrical machinery production.[7]

In the case of Brazil, which is the country which has accumulated the greatest share of European investments, 56 per cent of British investments are found in the manufacturing sectors, while the proportion for Germany is 90 per cent. In the motor industry German capital has undisputed pride of place: in 1978, Volkswagen's share of the passenger-car market in Brazil was 45 per cent, while the market share of Mercedes Benz was 56 per cent for lorries over 3 tons and 96 per cent for buses. VW of Brazil is the largest German investment abroad.

In Mexico, Germany is the European country with the largest share of FDI. Its overall percentage of total FDI for the period 1960-81 was 5.06 per cent, and, for the period 1977-81, German FDI in Mexico averaged 7.62 per cent annually. This compares with France's 1.14 per cent and Britain's 3.3 per cent annual average during the same period.[8] In 1984 Germany was the second largest investor in Mexico after the US, with 8.7 per cent of the total, followed by Japan (6.3 per cent) and Britain (3.1 per cent).[9]

As for France and Britain, the former has become a major source of investment in Brazil since 1973. The flows of French FDI amounted to FF 134 million in that year and rose steadily to FF 305 million in 1977, declining to FF 210 million in 1978.[10] Britain, too, though still concentrating its investment flows in countries in Africa and Asia, has shown a fair amount of interest in Latin America, particularly Chile and Mexico, where the flows of UK direct investment showed a particular increase in the period 1978-81 (see Table 4.2 overleaf).

It could be argued that any interest these European countries have in developments in Latin America is directly related to the need to protect their investments in the region. Although this consideration cannot be dismissed, it should be seen in the context of their overall pattern of outward investment. Of the three, Germany is the country which would stand to lose most from changes that were prejudicial to FDI in the area, given the considerable amount of capital it has invested in Latin America. For instance, the Deutsche-Sudamerikanische Bank of Hamburg reported that in 1983 14.8 per cent of West Germany's total direct investments abroad went to Latin America.[11] However, given the region's new investment climate, it does not seem likely that the countries within it will take a confrontation attitude towards foreign investment. Political risk considerations, too, need not be prominent in the industrialized countries' calculations. Europe should seize the opportunities that are now being presented for FDI in the region by a unique combination of firm long-term economic prospects and Latin America's economic opening up towards the North.

Table 4.2 UK outward direct investment attributable to UK companies (excluding oil companies, banks and insurance companies) in selected Third World countries, 1971–81 (£ mn)

Country	1971	1974	1978	1981
Latin America				
Argentina	58.8	70.7	107.5	95.2
Bahamas	43.8	86.5	70.2	107.5
Barbados*	–	7.8	16.7	23.0
Brazil	79.5	193.1	610.4	421.1
Chile	14.3	12.6	28.3	94.4
Colombia*	–	5.0	12.9	26.8
Jamaica	34.0	29.9	27.2	39.8
Mexico	52.0	51.3	97.2	277.9
Panama	6.5	8.1	15.8	27.1
Peru	3.9	3.8	4.0	6.7
Trinidad/				
Tobago	42.3	37.9	35.5˙	64.9
Uruguay	1.3	1.3	3.1	5.2
Venezuela	10.8	12.8	24.3	32.5
Total†	488.5	476.5	957.0	1,711.3
Africa and Asia				
Ghana	73.0	54.8	49.1	54.5
Kenya	60.5	88.1	178.2	208.0
Nigeria	155.6	198.7	479.1	638.4
Zimbabwe	78.7	113.6	216.9	479.4
Hong Kong	47.4	142.1	302.5	835.3
India	289.8	275.3	320.6	318.7
Malaysia	195.9	271.5	396.8	560.1
Singapore	19.5	53.7	207.2	419.6

Source: Business Statistics Office, *Business Monitor, Census of Overseas Assets, 1981* (HMSO, 1984).
*

†Caribbean, Central America and South America.

5 Debt

Background

The importance of the Latin American countries' position in the international financial markets was highlighted when the region's external debt difficulties suddenly claimed international attention in the summer of 1982. The magnitude of Latin America's outstanding foreign debts and the problems its countries were facing in servicing them became the concern of bankers and government officials alike.

The debt problems which today afflict most Latin American countries are the outcome of a series of international and external circumstances. During the 1960s, the bulk of external development finance for the region was provided by foreign direct investment and concessional flows; commercial bank lending at this stage was minimal. However, during the late 1960s and early 1970s, several events coincided to change the prevailing pattern. The first oil price hike of 1973 resulted in a steep rise in the oil import bills of the non-oil-producing developing nations. At the same time it provided banks with unprecedented amounts of funds from deposits by the oil exporters. The banks were willing to dispose of these funds and saw in the developing countries with a large potential for economic growth — many of them in Latin America — attractive alternative borrowers to the industrialized countries, which were undergoing economic recession.

At this time, the Latin American countries found themselves facing adverse circumstances: slow growth in their export markets, worsening terms of trade and higher oil bills. The temporary solution to these problems was to borrow from commercial banks: while world inflation was high, interest rates, though nominally higher than in the past, were still low and even negative in real terms. However, the Latin

American countries failed to make long-term adjustments to enable them to cope with developing trends in the international economy. They maintained overvalued exchange rates, which encouraged imports and the flight of capital, instead of stimulating exports and domestic savings; and they continued with large budget and current-account deficits, which were financed through foreign borrowing, mostly short-term and with floating interest rates.

The second oil shock, of 1979–80, exacerbated the situation. Oil prices rose again, export markets contracted, the terms of trade deteriorated even further and interest rates rose. Still the Latin American countries continued on the expansionary road. Oil exporters like Mexico and Venezuela benefited from the rise in oil prices, but even so remained as vulnerable as Brazil, Argentina and Chile to the industrialized countries' reactions (chiefly the tightening of their economic policies) to the state of the international economy. The increase in interest rates, raised primarily by US monetary and fiscal policies, was yet another external circumstance which affected the highly indebted Latin American countries, which were consequently forced to devote an increasing share of export revenues to the servicing of their debt. The situation eventually became unsustainable. In August 1982 Mexico, having exhausted its foreign reserves, declared its inability to go on servicing its debt. Mexico's declaration was the first in a series of unilateral *de facto* moratoria on debt repayment in other Latin American countries, the most notable being Brazil, Venezuela, Argentina, Chile and Ecuador.

During 1982 and 1983, many countries in the region were forced to reschedule their debts and most had to negotiate with the IMF in order to obtain standby loans and the necessary seal of approval that would allow them to renegotiate their commercial bank loans, as well as obtain credits from foreign governments and agencies.

The aim of this chapter is to assess how Latin America's debt problems have affected Europe. To what extent were British, French and German financial interests put in jeopardy as a result of their respective banks' exposure to Latin America? Have European reactions to Latin America's debt difficulties differed from those of the United States? What will the implications of the debt be for their economic, commercial and political interests in the region?

To a large extent the problems created by Latin American – or Third World – debt are shared by all the industrialized world. Its effects on the stability of the financial system and on international trade affect all major countries with a stake in them. The social and political consequences of the austerity measures that the Latin American countries will have to implement will be borne by the countries themselves, but if they result in social unrest and political instability, the effects on other countries, though unpredictable, could be serious.

Statistics on the debt levels of borrowing countries are readily available and commonly discussed, whether they refer to aggregates – oil importers and exporters, OPEC and non-OPEC countries, geographical regions – or to individual states. What is more difficult to find are figures that break down the loans into the countries of origin. This is understandable, since the great majority of loans are syndicated and involve a large number of banks. Moreover, as far as banking is concerned, it is difficult to speak in terms of nationality, since many banks are themselves partly subsidiaries of other banks. However, banking information has greatly improved in the past ten years or so, since bankers in most countries have to provide their central banks with information on cross-border exposure and the maturities of their loans. This information is coordinated by the Bank for International Settlements (BIS), and even if it is not standardized and not all banks publish their figures in detail, BIS information is sufficient for practical purposes. Table 5.1, based on BIS and IMF reports, provides a general picture of the exposure to Latin American countries of several banking groups. Although it is useful to have some idea of the aggregates for private banks of different countries, these data are not very informative on other equally important questions, such as the total exposure of national credit systems (including export credit agencies) or the quality of the portfolios.

European reactions to the crisis

The concern about the debtor countries' ability to service their debt was shared by bankers and governments on both sides of the Atlantic. However, there were differences of approach according to the nationality

Table 5.1 Outstanding debts and commitments by creditor banking group (before adjustment for guarantees), June 1983 (US $ mn)

Debt/creditor	US banks (A)	UK banks (B)	FRG banks (C)	French banks* (D)	A+B+C+D	All BIS-reporting banks	Total external debt, comparative estimates
Argentina	8,398	3,419	1,462	1,800	14,079	25,541	29,200
Brazil	20,539	8,296	2,023	7,000	37,858	62,778	85,450
Mexico	25,441	8,394	2,015	4,500	40,350	65,483	89,910
Venezuela	11,163	2,882	1,452	2,400	17,897	26,765	27,070
Chile	5,609	1,729	415	450	8,203	10,946	17,260
Colombia	3,331	800	118	–	4,249	6,632	10,280
Peru	2,626	763	72	700	4,161	5,305	9,360
Costa Rica	479	186	–	–	1,228	–	2,990
Ecuador	1,952	726	69	–	4,382	5,990	–
Total	79,538	27,195	7,626	16,950	–	–	–

Source: Amex Bank Review, *International Debt, Banks and the LDCs* (London, 1983).
*Data for December 1983.

of the banks concerned, the very dissimilar regulations they work under, the size of the bank and the extent of its exposure to the debt.

When the brunt of the crisis was felt in the summer of 1982, bankers and governments recognized how vital it was to avoid a sudden contraction of financial flows to the debt-ridden countries, because this would exacerbate their critical lack of liquidity and make the continued payment of interest impossible. The precarious stability of the international financial system had to be maintained, and a severe curtailment of credit would have had negative effects not only on the debtor countries, but on the system itself. The central banks of the creditor countries therefore undertook the task of persuading the banks under their control to keep the channels of credit open in order to help the debtor countries pay part of their overdue interest with fresh money. In Europe this was accomplished with comparative ease. However, the flow of net external credit was sharply reduced. The peak of financial flows to Latin America came in 1981, when the total amounted to $37.7 billion. This figure dropped to $19.2 billion in 1982 and to $4.4 billion by the end of 1983, turning Latin America into a net capital exporter.[1]

Although the reactions of individual countries to the debt crisis depended largely on specific banking regulations and accounting practices, the creditor countries achieved a considerable amount of coordination when they dealt with the immediate problems posed by the lack of liquidity of the debtor countries. This coordination took place in multilateral fora, such as the IMF, the BIS and the Paris Club. For instance, the BIS reported a great degree of cooperation among European central banks in providing important bridging loans to the Bank of Mexico and the Central Bank of Brazil.

The European reaction in the early stages of the crisis did not differ greatly from that of the United States. In general, though, the European banks could afford to be more flexible when dealing with the debt problems than could US banks, mainly because of their different banking regulations. How these can affect the attitude of banks towards the means of dealing with international debt problems is illustrated by the fact that European banks, though controlled by the banking authorities of their respective countries, are less subject to specific written regulations. American banking regulations are much more precise about when a loan is performing and when it is not: hence the overriding need of American banks to get interest paid on time so that their loans can pass the performance test. In fact, a split developed among the large US commercial banks over the issue of how to treat the Latin American debt problems in their accounts, and several of them postponed any decision until they received guidelines from the Securities and Exchange Commission.

US banking regulations were responsible for the almost desperate situation of American banks when Argentina seemed about to fall behind on the payment of interest on its loans in the spring of 1984. Had Argentina failed to meet the deadline on its interest payments, the US banks would have had to declare their loans non-performing, which would have had serious effects on accounting of profits and damaged the banks' position in the stock market. Another illustration of the effect of different banking regulations on attitudes towards the debt problem can be seen in the way European and US banks approach unconventional solutions. European bankers have accepted that in special cases developing countries can in principle be allowed to capitalize their interest payments. US banks, on the other hand, have shown a marked opposition to this type of partial solution.

However, although differences in national banking legislation had an important influence on approaches to the debt issues, perhaps the main reason for different reactions from different banks had to do with size. One important factor which has kept the financial system from showing signs of severe deterioration as a result of the debt crisis has been the flow of new money to enable debtors to meet their interest payments. Banking authorities on both sides of the Altantic used moral persuasion to convince banks to keep on lending. While it was in the interest of the highly exposed banks to grant new funds, the small, less exposed banks were reluctant to heed the advice of their central banks and argued that their freedom of action was being severely curtailed. As the managing director of a small Euromarket bank put it: 'For the first time in our history as independent bankers we have been robbed of our freedom of action in taking a decision on whether to make a loan or not . . . We were pretty much told by the deputy governor [of the Bank of England], "You have a bad loan, yet we are insisting you put more money into that situation in order to save the system."'[2]

But regardless of the extent of their exposure and the individual reactions of their banks, the governments of Britian, France and West Germany concurred to a large degree on how to sort out the crisis with the least possible disruption of the international financial and their own banking systems. However, there were some non-banking factors which tended to alter the picture from country to country, a clear example of which can be found in the case of the UK. There were special circumstances not directly related to the debt problem which Britain did not share with other creditors, namely, the Falklands conflict and the fact that Latin America as a region started receiving more attention as a result of it. These geopolitical considerations differentiated the British position from that of the United States, whose paramount interest was financial.

The British way of approaching the problem, which to a large extent was that followed by France and Germany, was that there were two aspects of debt which could not be dissociated from each other: the individual economic problems of the debtor countries, and their impact on the international financial system and, within that, on British banks. The Bank of England's primary aim was to preserve the stability of the British banking system, which was indirectly affected by those Latin American banks operating within it. A distinction should be made here between British banks that are wholly or mainly British-owned and those that are foreign-owned but registered in the UK. Latin American countries with banks registered in the UK are Brazil and Mexico. The fact that these two countries were on the top of the list of world debtors was a cause of concern for the Bank of England because of the uncertain future of their banking operations in the UK, and the effects of this on the British banking system, if they were not helped out of their difficulties.

The Bank of England helped Mexico to maintain the short-term external credit facilities of Mexican banks, a pattern that was also followed for Brazil. This involved the supervision of the banks working in the London market in order to avoid a withdrawal of deposits. The aim of the Bank of England was to stabilize inter-bank deposits so that the market could keep on functioning smoothly and provide banking flexibility. The Bank of England, utilizing its moral authority, persuaded British banks to maintain their credit lines. Some withdrawals occurred, but the Bank of England is reported to have received a high degree of cooperation from British banks, although, as has been mentioned above, there were some banks which were reluctant to follow suit.

In the case of the bridging loan requested by Argentina from the BIS in early 1983, the Bank of England, though not opposing it, refused to participate itself for political reasons. However, the British government was inconsistent in its attitude towards the participation of British private banks in a $1.1 billion credit for Argentina raised by 250 commercial banks around the same time. At first Mrs Thatcher did not object to British banks participating in this loan, despite strong opposition from parliament. At this stage she insisted that the British government was not standing in the way of this loan because it wanted to stave off a world banking crisis. However, later on, under mounting political pressure and with evidence that the Argentine junta had not lifted financial sanctions against British companies, the British government took a tougher stand on supporting commercial credits for Argentina. Because of the sanctions against British companies, Argentina ran into problems when trying to obtain an IMF-backed loan, since it is against IMF rules for members to engage in discriminatory practices. Finally, the British government insisted that participation by British banks in loans to Argentina should be conditional on Argentina's first having reached agreement with the IMF, and on the IMF's having ratified that Argentina had effectively lifted financial sanctions against the UK.

The case of France differs from that of Britain because of the peculiarities of the French banking system. The far-reaching nationalization programme of the Socialist government of February 1982 (which extended the 1945 takeover of the three main banks) could have facilitated a great degree of cooperation from French banks exposed in Latin America. However, in the case of the international sovereign debt, official pressure to maintain the flow of funds to debtor countries and to reschedule debts was not a big issue, perhaps because of the general belief that French banks were considerably less exposed in the 'problem countries' in Latin America. This belief, however, does not seem to be confirmed by the facts, as illustrated by Table 5.1, which shows French exposure in the four major Latin American countries exceeding that of Germany. Figures from Mexico's central bank indicate that at the end of 1982 France's credits to Mexico's public sector amounted to $4.3 billion dollars, or 7.3 per cent of Mexico's public debt,[3] and certainly in the case of export credit French officials seem to think that in Mexico they were more exposed than other countries.

In Germany there was a directive from the Bundesbank that the German banks should continue lending. Some have argued that German banks were readier than others to compromise and accept smaller spreads over and above libor.* This was an important concession, since at one point the Latin American countries were paying interest three percentage points above Libor. This was remarked upon by the chairman of the US Council of Economic Advisers, Martin Feldstein, who expressed the hope that banks would lower their lending rates to the Latin American countries.[4]

As further evidence of the flexible attitude in Germany, it has also been stated that German banks were more open to unconventional alternatives for solving the debt problem. These alternatives included debt-to-equity conversions (in the case of private debts) or the capitalization of interests rates. Although the German banks did not specify which of these methods they preferred, it has been claimed that they were more interested in managing the debt problem in the long term.

Apart from the political factor in the British approach to the debt problem (in the specific case of Argentina), there seemed to be general agreement among the leaders of the European and other industrialized countries that the debt problem called for a collective approach. This was demonstrated at the London Economic Summit of June 1984. The joint communiqué emphasized that the debtor countries needed the industrialized nations' help to make the necessary economic and financial policy changes. To this effect the leaders agreed to support the IMF's role in monitoring the adjustment programmes; to encourage further cooperation between the IMF and the World Bank; to foster economic development in the medium and long term; to help debtor countries improve their position by encouraging multiyear rescheduling of commercial debts; and to 'negotiate similarly in respect of debts of government agencies.' Finally, the Summit's action programme pledged

---

*Spreads are the difference between what borrowers pay on bank loans and the rates that banks pay for the deposits which fund these loans. One of these rates is known as Libor: the London interbank offered rate.

to encourage the flow of long-term investment and recognized the need for developed countries to make their markets more open to exports from developing countries.

This statement of good intentions, however, has not been strictly adhered to in practice. While commercial banks have adopted a multi-year approach to the renegotiation of their loans to the Latin American countries (in particular to Mexico and Venezuela), the governments of the industrial countries have not moved in parallel with the banks. The first test the governments faced after the June 1984 Summit was the renegotiation of official loans to Mexico. In this case, the governments refused to renegotiate in tandem with the banks in the Paris Club, their forum for the negotiation of debts on credits extended or guaranteed by official government agencies. The main argument of the governments for not negotiating with Mexico within the Paris Club was that a precondition of this was usually the suspension of an officially guaranteed trade credit, which was not the case with Mexico.[5] This argument was put forward despite the fact that Mexico had succeeded in achieving a multiyear rescheduling of $48.7 billion of its public debt, with a maturity of 14 years and an interest of only 1.1 per cent above money market rates on average. Mexico's unprecedentedly good terms for refinancing its sovereign debt set the pattern for other Latin American debtors.

The other big debtor, Brazil, also encountered difficulties in the negotiation of its debts with official creditors. Negotiations with the Paris Club were held in 1984, but by the end of that year no agreement had been reached. One reason for this was Brazil's delay in reaching agreement with the IMF, and one of the Paris Club policies is not to reschedule until this has been accomplished. Within the Paris Club, it has only been Ecuador and Costa Rica among the Latin American countries that have achieved multiyear reschedulings of their officially guaranteed commercial debts.

The degree of success in handling the international debt crisis will necessarily depend on the coordinated actions of three important actors: the IMF, the commercial banks and the governments. The effects of the economic policies of both debtor and creditor nations are closely interrelated. If the Latin American countries are unsuccessful in managing their external debts, this will be reflected in varying degrees in the industrial countries. Consequently, the United States, Europe and the rest of the industrial world all experience common problems in relation to Latin America. So far the international banking system has been able to survive the first debt shock. However, the effects on the trade sectors of the industrial countries are still being felt. It is in the interest of the creditor countries to reduce trade protectionism in order to allow the Latin American – and other Third World – countries to earn sufficient foreign exchange to keep servicing their debts. But the burden of debt payments should also be carefully considered, because of its long-term implications. The Latin American countries will not be able to continue acting as net exporters of capital indefinitely. The stringent economic conditions under which they are currently acting will have to be eased, in order to avoid a further collapse in the not too distant future. The threat of a possible regression to the 1982 situation has not vanished yet.

An area generally overlooked by the creditor nations' governments is the political dimension of the debt problem, which has so far been tackled only from the financial point of view. One of the aspects of the political dimension is how the adjustment programmes being carried out by the Latin American countries – and other debtors – will affect the political stability of the region. This leads naturally to a consideration of the political importance of Latin America for Europe.

6 Political interests

Overview

The political dimension of Europe's interest in Latin America presents a more complex picture than one might expect, in view of Europe's general lack of presence in the region, and indeed of the marginal strategic and geopolitical significance of Latin America to Europe. Such complexity is perhaps due to the importance Europe attaches to its relationship with the United States, its senior partner in the Atlantic Alliance, together with the USA's special relationship with the Latin American republics.

Until relatively recently Latin America was regarded by West European countries as being within the exclusive sphere of influence of the US. American hegemony exhibited the capacity and the influence to solve, by diplomatic or military means, problems which threatened the stability of the region. The Latin American countries in general closely followed the US line in international affairs. Their defence and security were guaranteed by the inter-American institutions — the OAS (Organization of American States) and TIAR (Treaty of Inter-American Reciprocal Assistance) — under the direct tutelage of the United States.

However, circumstances started to change a decade or so ago. The US began to lose its tight grip on Latin America, as a result of such international disasters as Vietnam and the abortive attempt to rescue the hostages in Iran. Domestic problems like Watergate further undermined its credibility, and possibly it took its influence in the region for granted. Latin America, which had achieved a sustained rate of economic growth and was the most dynamic region in the Third World in economic terms, began to seek a more independent and active role in regional as well as global affairs.[1] About the same time, the old order in Central

America started to crumble under pressure from the forces of change.

Instability in Central America became a concern not only for the US, whose declining influence was apparent in the wake of the Sandinista victory in Nicaragua, but also indirectly for the European countries. If events in Central America forced a full-scale intervention, the US would be unable to focus its attention on other areas of potential conflict, such as Europe, Asia or the Middle East. The strategic value of the region — including the Panama Canal and the sea lanes in the Caribbean and the Gulf of Mexico — also had to be borne in mind. Vast amounts of commercial trade travel on these routes, which provide a vital link for the US with other regions in the world. The Caribbean area is the natural channel for as much as 40 per cent of US supplies to Western Europe. Furthermore, the increasing instability in the Third World, and particularly in Cental America, has elicited different responses from the different members of NATO, and 'out-of-NATO-area' crises generally are potentially divisive and could affect the US presence in Europe.

From the Latin American perspective, the power vacuum left by the declining influence of the United States prompted the governments of the region (and certain political groups in opposition) to seek new partners and allies. Some were found within Latin America itself in the more assertive regional actors — Mexico, Venezuela or Cuba. But Europe, too, presented a viable means of counteracting the US and what was left of its once overwhelming influence in the area. Moreover, European moral and material support seemed to have the advantage of being more 'neutral', with fewer strings attached, than had been the case with the United States. The reactivation of the European/Latin American relationship, so close during the nineteenth century, was received with mixed feelings by the US. Although closer economic relations between the two regions gained support and even encouragement from Washington, Europe's political interest in Latin America was less welcome.[2]

The NATO context

The European governments have two political interests in common in Latin America: the stability of the region, and the maintenance or development of its democratic institutions. These oversimplified objectives require some qualification. The stability of Latin America is not Europe's direct concern; its aim is rather to keep the US free from unwanted distractions in areas that do not directly bear upon European defence needs. Furthermore, Europe's support for democracy in Latin America is more rhetorical than real (with some exceptions, such as the last Labour government in the UK, which broke off diplomatic relations with Chile after Pinochet's coup). European governments have not felt particularly uneasy about doing business with dictatorial regimes in Latin America – or elsewhere – as will be seen in the country-by-country analysis. It seems that whenever European interests conflict with an opportunity to make concessions in order to strengthen democracy or with the need to put pressure on authoritarian regimes, the defence of European interests prevails.

One important factor that determines official European policies towards Latin America is membership of multilateral organizations – NATO and the EC – which are vital to Europe's strategic, economic and political interests. Europe's relationship with the United States within the Atlantic Alliance has been one of close cooperation. However, its recent tendency towards greater independence was clearly illustrated when it decided to buy gas from the Soviet Union and cooperate in the building of the gas pipeline, despite American objections. Europe is also increasingly determined to play a more assertive role in its own defence and security arrangements.[3] Although the survival of the alliance and the cooperation agreements with the US are in no way jeopardized by these initiatives, they do nonetheless point to Europe's greater detachment from the US in international affairs.

This greater assertiveness on Europe's part has been particularly marked with regard to Latin American and Caribbean affairs, in which it has frequently shown considerable opposition to American policies and actions. Central America and Grenada are two cases in point. The Grenada operation badly bruised relations between Europe and the US. There was resentment not only about the lack of consultation (especially in Britain, because of Grenada's status as a Commonwealth country and Britain's 'special relationship' with the US), but also about the violation of the principle of sovereignty. President Reagan's most loyal ally in Europe, the British Prime Minister, who had referred to the

United States as 'the final guarantor of freedom in Europe', stated a few days after the invasion: 'If you are going to pronounce a new law that wherever Communism reigns against the will of the people . . . the United States shall enter, then we are going to have really terrible wars in the world.'[4] Britain was not alone in opposing the invasion: France, Germany, Belgium, Italy and the Netherlands also voiced their condemnation. Relations between the United States and its European allies were so damaged that a senior American official, Deputy Secretary of State Kenneth Dam, was sent to Europe to explain US motives and to ease the strains in the alliance. There were fears in the US that the Grenada invasion would interfere with, delay or jeopardize the deployment of American medium-range missiles in Europe.

The wave of anti-American feeling caused by the Grenada invasion was not unwelcome to Moscow. The Kremlin hoped that the invasion would weaken European confidence in US leadership in foreign affairs and threaten the deployment of cruise and Pershing II missiles. The Kremlin's assessment was partially correct, but Europe's lack of trust in the US did not go that far.[5] Although events in Grenada, and Reagan's policy towards Central America generally, added fuel to the fire of those who were protesting that Europe was no more than Washington's 'nuclear hostage', the European governments managed to weather the storm of anti-American feeling, and, in the end, NATO's defence plans remained intact.

The EC context

After the European Community was created, its member countries developed a mild interest in Latin America which focused mainly on political change in the region, not least because of the Cuban revolution. This concern with political developments gained more substance when Latin America began to be discussed in the European Parliament, whose direct acquaintance with the region dates back to the establishment of the Inter-Parliamentary Conferences in 1970. The new composition of the European Parliament, elected directly since 1979, has helped to reinforce attention to the region, since some political groups among the MEPs have Latin American connections. Latin America has also been receiving more attention in the media and from the public, with the result that MEPs have been concerned with human rights and the evolution of the democratic process in various Latin American countries.

Perhaps because of this closer contact and increased knowledge of the area, the EC as a collectivity has adopted less ambiguous positions on such issues as Central America, Chile, the Andean Pact and SELA than its often vacillating member countries, with the possible exception of Germany. It is also interesting to note that its approach to Latin America as a whole has tended to tilt more openly against US policy than has been possible for its individual members, which are anxious not to damage their bilateral relations with the US. This is one of the advantages that could be gained from a collective approach to the region.

On two issues that have recently dominated international attention the EC has shown a remarkable degree of cohesion: namely, Central America and the Falklands. The triangular relationship between Europe, Latin America and the United States became strained by an event that, quite unexpectedly, brought Latin America closer to Europe's attention: the sudden military confrontation between two countries of major significance in different US alliances. The Falklands dispute dramatically illustrated how interdependent Europe and Latin America are in international affairs. A belated European concern to know the region better and follow developments there more closely started to develop. Indeed, a little more knowledge of Latin American politics and character (and military!) would have been useful before the British/Argentine conflict.

For Latin America, the Falklands war, and the US attitude and actions in it, were a signal that the USA's main allies were to be found across the Atlantic and not to the south.[6] It also demonstrated that the inter-American security arrangements which had guaranteed the region's security since the end of World War II were inoperative and void of any practical significance. The unity of the EC with regard to Latin America was also in evidence during the Falklands, at least on the surface, when it came to imposing economic sanctions on Argentina. Denmark, Ireland and Italy were the most reluctant to go ahead, for different reasons, and the last two withdrew from this action. Denmark felt it should uphold its position that national decision-making had precedence over European; Italy was mindful of its special economic interests and its traditional and emotional ties with Argentina; and Ireland's withdrawal was perhaps a sign of its opposition to UK colonialism. Although France's economic interests were also affected, it seems that the French were instrumental in getting agreement on sanctions.

European 'unity' on the Falklands has managed to survive. When a resolution urging the parties in conflict to resume negotiations was voted on at the UN General Assembly in 1983 and 1984, the European partners supported Britain by abstaining. In the 1984 vote, this unity was preserved despite President Alfonsín's personal attempt to persuade Italy and France to support the resolution during his European tour shortly beforehand.

Europe has been in constant disagreement with the US over the Central American crisis, although the European countries' positions have not been so uniformly against the US as they were in the Grenada affair. The approach adopted by the EC — with Britain going along reluctantly and being more sympathetic to the US — differs widely from that of the Reagan administration. The EC sees as the root of the problems there the degree of social injustice and repression and the lack of political participation, rather than Soviet and Cuban designs. There is also a common European position that would oppose US military intervention in Central America, or indeed in any other country. The European Community has therefore sought to adopt an independent policy in Central America to help bring about a negotiated solution that would diminish the possibility of a US intervention.

The EC's actions and pronouncements on Central America have been firm. One example of this was the statement at the June 1983 Summit at Stuttgart, when the EC distanced itself from Reagan's Central American policy by declaring that the area's problems 'cannot be solved by military means, but *only* by a solution springing from the region and respecting the principles of non-interference and the inviolability of frontiers'.[7] In September 1983, on German and Dutch initiatives, some foreign ministers of the EC and the President of the Commission met with their counterparts in the Contadora countries to discuss the possibility of initiating political negotiations among all the parties in conflict in Central America.*

*In January 1983 the foreign ministers of Colombia, Mexico, Panama and Venezuela met on the island of Contadora in the Gulf of Panama to launch a proposal for a negotiated solution to the Central American conflict.

Another example of the EC's commitment to a policy towards Central America independent of the US came almost a year later, in the unprecedented meeting of the foreign secretaries of the Ten, and of Spain and Portugal as potential members, in San José de Costa Rica, to discuss the crisis. They were joined by the foreign ministers of the five Central American countries and those of the Contadora group. The United States was not invited, although neither was Cuba. The meeting came after a peace-seeking mission by Costa Rican President Monge, and it was the result of joint efforts by Monge and the German Foreign Minister, Hans-Dietrich Genscher. The German government saw itself as the promoter of this meeting, and, interestingly, the Genscher statement on it declared that the cooperation sought with the region would be similar to that established between the Community and ASEAN, and reiterated that that, too, had been a German initiative.

In spite of these collective EC responses to the general thrust of US policy in Central America, each member of the Community has adopted a different individual approach. There has been divergence on the degree of opposition to US policies, depending on the nature and political orientation of the governments, and on the strength of the parliamentary oppositions and subgovernmental actors, in each country.

The most notable case of official disagreement with the United States was provided by France's Socialist government, especially at the beginning of the Mitterrand administration. In August 1981 France issued a joint communiqué with Mexico recognizing the armed opposition in El Salvador (the FMLN) and its political wing (the FDR) as legitimate forces. Moreover, it matched radical words with radical action: it provided arms to Nicaragua; it did not send observers to El Salvador's elections; it forcefully condemned the US mining of Nicaraguan ports; and it offered minesweepers to Nicaragua. All these activities infuriated Washington, but, with the passage of time and the deterioration of the Socialist position domestically, the French government moderated its position. France also feels less justified in opposing US actions in Central America now that its own military forces are embroiled in the civil war in Chad.

The French attitude contrasts sharply with that of the UK, whose Conservative government has followed a policy more in line with US wishes: not offering aid to Nicaragua; sending official observers to

International Herald Tribune 3/8/83
'Reagan's moves in CA make Atlantic partners uneasy'

elections in El Salvador and not to Nicaragua; generally keeping a low profile in Central America; and certainly not supporting the forces of change in the area. Britain's Labour opposition, however, has consistently taken a more critical view of US policies in Central America and has denounced official British policy as a mirror image of that of the US.[8]

It is perhaps in Germany that the widest spectrum of opinions and actions has emerged with regard to Central America and US policies towards it. Official attitudes have been more cautious than those of the German political parties and their respective foundations. Under the Social Democratic government of Helmut Schmidt, Germany's policies towards Latin America in general and Central America in particular created tensions with Washington. However, with the coming to power of Chancellor Kohl, the ideological bent of German official policy towards Central America changed, notwithstanding the fact that Liberal Foreign Minister Genscher, who has progressive views on the subject, remained in the new government. The Christian Democrats now had the upper hand in the formulation of foreign policy, and support for Nicaragua and the FDR in El Salvador waned. Instead, the Germans gave their support to the moderate Christian Democrats in the region, such as José Napoleón Duarte.

Country-by-country analysis

Because Britain, France and Germany do not place Latin America particularly high on their political agendas, any attention they have given to the region has tended to be diluted and erratic. It is not surprising, therefore, that there is currently no coherent medium- or long-term policy towards Latin America, and it does not look as though this situation will improve in the future. However, the very fact that the region is relatively unimportant to European economic, political and strategic interests means that it has been used for political experimentation. Policies have changed according to the ideological preferences of the party in power, a fact that has been remarked upon by the Americans. An illustration of this, with particular reference to Central America, is the following statement: 'In the absence of vital interests, some European governments and political parties have responded to domestic political interests in placating left-wing sectors and displaying independence from the US.'[9]

In fact the European actors most attracted to the area and with the clearest idea of their political interests, and therefore with a coherent policy, are not governments as such, but subgovernmental political groups, like the Social and Christian Democrats, who have effectively established their presence in Latin America from grass-roots level up. In this respect Germany's transnational relations with the region have been by far the most active.

For France and, even more so, Britain, relations with Latin America have reflected colonial responsibilities. Britain went to war with Argentina to defend the sovereignty of its dependency in the South Atlantic. On the other hand, Britain does not share with France and Germany another political link which comes more naturally to countries on the Continent. There are important affinities between French and German political movements and those in Latin America, perhaps more so in the case of Germany. In France only the Socialists and Communists have sister parties in Latin America, and Latin American Communism is much less potent a political force than it is in France. However, Germany's political movements, Social and Christian Democracy, are at the forefront of Latin American politics.

France

The French presence in Latin America has been steadily declining ever since its peak in the nineteenth century. Certainly, since World War II, whatever French influence was left in countries other than its colonies has been eclipsed by that of the US, both politically and culturally. However, although the French government has kept a low profile in the Americas, it is evident from the size of official financial flows to Martinique, Guadeloupe and French Guiana that these territories represent its most important interest in the region. The large sums involved, which make French possessions the world's largest per capita recipients of official aid, are also an indication that France has no intention of abandoning its colonies in the Americas, which were incorporated into French territory in 1946.[10] Of the three, French Guiana has particular importance, in that ever since Algerian independence it has provided France with its main launching-site for non-military rockets and a suitable base for space research.[11]

It has been argued that French concern about the instability in Central America and the Caribbean, especially during the Giscard d'Estaing administration, centred on the possibility that the conflicts in the area might have spill-over effects on the French DOM.[12] Therefore the central aim of France's relations with the Latin American governments was the stability of the area and the means to achieve it. Also during Giscard's administration, it was thought that a way to maintain stability in the region was to keep an open dialogue with governments in Latin America regardless of their ideology. This stance was justified on the grounds that France was providing an alternative to their possible attachment to one of the two superpower blocs, which would only foster political tensions in the area and increase instability. It is suprising that this rationale of providing alternatives to superpower alignment remained virtually unchanged under the Socialist administration that succeeded Giscard's.

But change did follow the Socialists' assumption of power in 1981. Whereas, during Giscard's administration, France favoured relations with moderate governments which were against the coming to power of progressive parties, the French Socialist government of François Mitterrand came out in favour of change, and of providing support for the leftist elements in the region. On assuming power Mitterrand cooled relations with Chile, but did not break them, and imposed an embargo on French arms exports negotiated under his predecessor. Giscard's justification for maintaining relations with authoritarian regimes in Latin America was that France did not recognize governments but states, and that it was against French policy to intervene in the internal affairs of other countries.

Indeed, the election of Mitterrand as president augured changes in French foreign policy in general. The Socialist electoral platform highlighted the importance of Third World problems for overall international stability. In the Socialists' perception, the East/West conflict would intensify not in the traditional field, Europe, but in the South. They therefore favoured increased aid to less developed areas and solidarity with national liberation movements. If the West did not lend a helping hand to those peoples fighting against political oppression and poverty, they would take up arms and turn to others, i.e. the

Soviet Union. 'Et nous finissons par pousser dans le camp adverse des gens qui ne sont pas des adversaires naturels de l'Occident, mais qui le deviennent par la logique de la situation que nous les imposons.'[13]

French Socialists, with their traditional world view of anti-militarism, pacifism and internationalism, naturally opposed the US, whose international policies were regarded as being aimed at maintaining the status quo. But once in power, the Socialists, under Mitterrand's leadership, adopted policies foreign to their ideological principles. Support for the US, particularly within the NATO framework, was strong, even more so than under Giscard. In fact Mitterrand criticized Giscard for keeping aloof from the European missile debate. During his visit to Germany in January 1983, perhaps worried by the neutralist drift in West German public opinion and the increasing instability in Europe, Mitterrand expressed France's full support for the Atlantic Alliance.[14]

This Atlanticist position contrasted with the policy (more in line with Socialist rhetoric) which France adopted towards the less developed areas, which were not vital to France's defence and security. In Latin America France sought to strengthen its links with Mexico and Venezuela, and to follow a policy in Central America which favoured change and was thus opposed to US perceptions and policies on 'stabilization' plans for the crisis there. The appointment of Régis Debray as foreign affairs adviser to Mitterrand promised a more active, and enlightened, policy towards Latin America, given Debray's substantial experience of the region, his close acquaintance with Che Guevara and his critical role as the theorist of Latin American guerrilla movements.

As already mentioned, the French commitment to a radical policy in Latin America gradually became more moderate. When domestic economic and political issues began to acquire increasing urgency, demanding the full attention of the French government, it became clear that there was a limited amount of attention that France could give to issues and areas of secondary importance.

Britain

The coming to power of the Conservatives under Margaret Thatcher in 1979 brought about a more drastic change in British policy towards Latin America than was the case with France's change of government. The thrust of Conservative policy was to normalize relations with

Latin America, which meant reinstating in Chile and Argentina the British ambassadors who had been withdrawn under Labour. In the case of Chile, Labour's decision was taken in 1975 following the disclosure of the imprisonment and torture of Dr Sheila Cassidy and William Beausire by the Chilean junta. In the case of Argentina, the decision followed shots fired at the British research ship, HMS Shackleton, early in 1976 near the Falklands. Relations with Argentina were then maintained at a reduced level by the Labour government, because of the takeover by the military in March of that year and the subsequent violations of human rights.

The Conservative government sent an ambassador to Argentina in July 1979, and relations were fully restored. This decision, in contrast with the decision to send an ambassador to Chile, did not arouse significant opposition in Britain, 'largely because of the unfamiliarity of the Argentinian situation to most of the British labour movement'.[15] As with France, the justification was that the maintenance of diplomatic relations was a technical matter and did not imply the endorsement of these countries' regimes. The normalization of relations with Chile included the renewal of full ECGD coverage, which had been curtailed under Labour.

Again in common with France, the UK's relations with Latin America are determined to a great extent by its colonial presence in the area. Thus, the Caribbean region is far more important politically for the UK than the mainland, since a large number of independent Commonwealth countries and dependent territories are located there. Although many of them have become independent, links with Britain have remained important, not least because there has been substantial emigration from the Caribbean to the UK.

Britain's colonial policy has been rather confused. During the 1960s and 1970s it gave the impression that it wanted to reduce its colonial responsibilities. At one point it was even accused of wanting to hand over British Honduras (Belize) and the Falklands to Guatemala and Argentina respectively. The responsibility for British Guiana came to an end when it gained independence as Guyana in 1966. This brought about accusations from the Venezuelan government that Britain had granted independence in order to evade responsibility in the unresolved territorial dispute between Venezuela and Guyana.

85

Political interests

Belize's independence in 1981 relieved Britain of another colonial burden, although it has maintained a military presence there to guard Belizean territorial integrity against possible aggressions from Guatemala, which has refused to recognize Belizean independence. The size of the military presence – 1,800 men, and light aircraft and armoured support – is not very significant, but it is an important symbol. Britain's relations with Guatemala are mainly determined by the issue of Belize, and it has remained opposed to the possible resumption of arms supplies from the US to Guatemala.

The Falklands have presented Britain with a thornier problem than Belize and Guyana, which, because of territorial size and population, were well able to become independent countries. Independence was a relatively easy way for Britain to divest itself of these colonies while at the same time retaining a special link with them through the Commonwealth. But it is hard to imagine a viable independent Falkland Islands, with their 1,800 or so inhabitants, and in any case the Falklanders have not wanted to change their status but have wished to remain British. Any departure from dependence on the UK could well result in an increasing dependence on Argentina, an unwanted consequence, at least for the Islanders. The problem has been complicated by a persistently bellicose attitude on the part of Argentina, which wants to regain the Islands, as well as a lack of progress in negotiations about their status. The Argentine decision to occupy the Falklands, which led to the military confrontation, makes it difficult to turn the clock back and restart negotiations without the intransigence that now exists on both sides over even the discussion of sovereignty. There had been several occasions when negotiations between the two countries had led to agreement that Argentina's sovereignty over the islands would be recognized once the British government was entirely satisfied that the Falklanders' interests would be secure.

Events turned the Falklands into an emotive political issue for the new democratic government in Argentina as well as for the US government. In Britain, the extravagant economic costs of maintaining a Fortress Falklands policy are still compensated for by the symbolic political value of British military victory and the recovery of threatened territory. But this symbolism is wearing off, and the controversy surrounding the sinking of the Belgrano has engendered doubts about the British government's sincerity in seeking a negotiated solution at the time of the armed conflict. For Argentina, the Falklands are a leitmotiv of national pride and a strong symbol of national unity. Resolution of the dispute could help bolster the new democracy, which is facing so many problems on other fronts.

There is widespread agreement that successive British governments have tried to disencumber themselves of the Falklands. As early as March 1967 the British government 'for the first time stated formally to Argentina that they would be prepared to cede sovereignty over the Islands under certain conditions provided that the wishes of the Falklanders were respected.'[16] However, the UK's willingness to consider the transfer of sovereignty was thwarted by very well organized lobbying on behalf of the Islanders. Indeed, as the Foreign Affairs Committee Report on the Falkland Islands makes clear, 'under insistent pressure from the Falklands and in the House of Commons, successive British governments found themselves obliged to lay increasing emphasis on the wishes of the Falkland Islanders and discovered those wishes to be so apparently inflexible.'[17]

British policy on the Falklands is unlikely to change while the Thatcher government remains in power. The new Falklands constitution and the recent inauguration of the airport at Port Stanley seem to confirm this. One current of opinion believes that a valuable opportunity was lost for Britain to negotiate with Argentina over the Falklands when the transition from a military to a popularly elected government took place in Buenos Aires late in 1983. The justification for British inaction when Alfonsín became president was that there was no guarantee that the civilian government would last long enough to make any agreement long-lived. This argument, however, is weak, since any such agreement could have been made conditional on the permanence of a democratically elected government.

Nevertheless, the political reasons for keeping current British policy on the Falklands intact may well vanish after the next general election, which takes place in 1988 at the latest. If the Conservatives are then no longer governing the country, a revision of the Falklands policy may be expected. At present, however, there is no real internal pressure on the British government to find a long-term solution to the conflict, although such pressure may be forthcoming from outside if the European countries begin to waver in their solidarity with Britain in international fora. This solidarity is likely to be eroded as time goes by, and, when the issue is finally negotiated, Britain may have lost much of its partners' support.

Germany

Of the three countries examined, Germany is the one that attaches most political importance to Latin America. Its presence in the area through its political parties, foundations and churches has had a major impact on Latin American internal political developments. This situation contrasts sharply with the almost total absence of the two other countries' political movements in the region and raises the question of what the motivations are behind the strong unofficial German political commitment in Latin America. Some people take the view that this political presence can be regarded as a means of gaining an advantage over other European countries in the region in the promotion of trade and industry. Others argue that since the end of World War II Germany has tried to overcome a feeling of international isolation by establishing close friendly relations with other geographical areas, especially in the Third World. However, neither of these views does justice to the complexity of Germany's motivations for increasing its political activities in Latin America.

There are four main interrelated elements which should be considered when assessing Germany's role in Latin America. First, it never played a colonial role in the region. Second, its partition and political position in the postwar period left it in a state of relative isolation, which in turn led it to seek out possible partners and alliances with countries outside Europe. Third, it considers Latin America to be the area in the Third World with most economic potential and the one whose political and cultural values are most akin to its own. Fourth, it believes that its democratic future depends on a democratic world friendly to Germany.

Most of Germany's political activities in the region are not carried out at the official level, but by subgovernmental organizations and groups. Moreover, German observers of Latin American affairs have noted with concern the discrepancy between the high level of transnational activity by non-governmental groups and the low profile of government policy.[18] The recommendation that official German policy towards Latin America should match the degree of importance and involvement of the transnational organizations perhaps overlooks the fact that allowing subgovernmental actors to take the initiative in the establishment of relations with Latin American groups in government and opposition has had the important advantage of letting Germany secure a political presence in the area without having to pay a price in terms of explicit conflict of interest with the United States. That is, non-official involvement is a freer form of action.

There are four political foundations (Stiftungen) in Germany, the Friedrich Ebert, Konrad Adenauer, Hans Seidel and Friedrich Naumann foundations. These are affiliated to the four political parties, the Social Democratic Party (SPD), the Christian Democratic Union (CDU), the Christian Social Union (CSU, the Bavarian section of the CDU), and the Free Democratic Party (FDP) respectively. They are supported with funds from the federal government, regardless of which party is in power, but they are also recipients of private donations. German leaders and politicians believe that German political culture has a lot in common with that of Latin America. The Social Democratic, Christian Democratic and Liberal parties are convinced that they have their ideological counterparts there, more than in any other area of the Third World. But perhaps because of Latin America's Christian tradition, and the relative strength of the Christian Democratic movement in the region, the CDU and its foundation, the Konrad Adenauer Stiftung, have found in Latin America fertile ground for dialogue and political collaboration, and willing recipients of aid. The Konrad Adenauer foundation devotes 50 per cent of its funds to Latin America.

Most of the German foundations present their objectives in Latin America as part of a concerted effort to defeat totalitarian regimes, of both the left and the right, but in terms of *realpolitik* it could be argued that this channelling of funds to the region has the ulterior motive of securing political and economic advantages. The German foundations admit that a close acquaintance with the political groups in power (or in opposition but which could eventually come to power) in a given country may help secure contracts for German firms, but they deny that this is the real purpose of their work in Latin America. In any case, it is stated, the amount of funding and the efforts spent helping local political parties and lending assistance to programmes of self-help and other activities involve far greater costs than the benefits that a good business contract could secure. The justifying theme behind the activities of each of the German political foundations is that Germany is in search of like-minded partners so that it can boost democratic forces. It is in this area that German political parties and their respective foundations believe Europe has a role to play in Latin America, namely, helping to promote pluralistic democratic regimes.

The CDU's activities and those of its foundation have concentrated on the countries which have a Christian Democratic tradition. Thus, in Chile, the CDU has opposed the Pinochet regime and has supported the democratization process by bolstering the Alianza Democrática, which is headed by the leader of the Christian Democratic Party. Likewise it has given support to Napoleón Duarte in El Salvador and to Arnulfo Arias in Panama. In other countries the CDU has avoided involvement. In Guatemala the CDU believes that the political structure still impedes the participation of certain groups and does not allow genuine pluralism, and so it is not present in that country. Mexico and Argentina are two countries in which the CDU has not found like-minded political groups, and it believes that official Mexican policy supports radical views with regard to the Third World which run counter to CDU ideology.

The Ebert Stiftung has sought to give support to parties with a Social Democratic leaning, and, like the CDU, the SPD has channelled funds to parties with a similar orientation to its own. The most controversial of the Ebert foundations' activities has been the financial support of the Sandinistas prior to their overthrow of Somoza.

The SPD has another non-governmental organization through which it can direct its political activities: the Socialist International (SI).[19] The SI decision to participate actively in developments in Latin America was taken at a meeting held in Caracas in 1976. The same year saw the election of Willy Brandt as the president of the SI, and his concern with North/South issues meant that the priority for SI activities would be the Third World, within which Latin America occupied a special place, since developments in Central America were threatening a major international conflict. In 1979 the SI created a committee for Latin America and the Caribbean under the presidency of José Francisco

Peña Gómez of the Dominican Republic, and in November 1980 a Committee for the Defence of the Nicaraguan Revolution was created under the presidency of Felipe González.

The SI's influence in developments in Central America has been extensive. It has provided more external support for the Sandinista regime than any other Western government or organization. However, changes in the Sandinista regime's orientation and the stifling of pluralist methods have led the SI to reappraise its initial enthusiam for the Nicaraguan revolution.

In their attempts to exert a political influence in the area, Christian and Social Democrats have often come into conflict with the United States, especially in Central America. Although it has been stated that the US welcomes the support and training in political development of the moderate forces in the region by these two European political movements, it also believes they have contributed significantly to the internationalization of the Central American conflict, and to the consequent increase in instability. However, it is also true that German *official* policy has run into some difficulty with Washington, particularly after 1969, when the German government decided to stress its support for change in order to achieve long-term stability in the region as a whole. It believed that the stifling of reforms would eventually lead to serious problems, and this view was shared by the CDU and the SPD.

Germany's general attitude towards Latin America reflects this conviction. Large segments of public opinion welcomed the Socialist experiment in Chile under the Unidad Popular government headed by Salvador Allende, and Germany had a generous policy towards Chilean refugees in the aftermath of the military coup. It has kept a prudent distance from Pinochet's junta and has resisted pressures from the US to warm up its relations with Chile and Paraguay. Indeed, of the two main disagreements between Bonn and Washington, one has been directly related to German economic interests in Latin America, with specific reference to US opposition to the German/Brazilian agreement on nuclear energy, and the other has been Germany's interference and support for change in Central America. American/German relations became very tense over differing perceptions of the Central American crisis, especially when Chancellor Schmidt was in power.

*　　　*　　　*

Latin America's overall political importance in the international arena has grown enormously in the last few years, and it has therefore been argued that it would be in Europe's interest to adopt a coherent medium- and long-term policy for dealing with Latin America as a region and with its individual countries. A convenient point of departure for elaborating such a policy is to assess what Europe's primary political concerns are in the region, at both the collective and the individual level.

The two main political issues which have attracted European attention to Latin America have been the South Atlantic conflict (and the state of British relations with Argentina and their bearing on European relations with Latin America in general) and the instability in Central America (and the effects this can have on European defence and Atlantic relations).

The armed confrontation in the South Atlantic badly shook relations between Europe and Latin America. Since then, token gestures aimed at improving this state of affairs have taken place, for instance the signing of a cooperation agreement between the European Community and the Andean Pact, and increased Community aid funds for Central America. The increase in economic assistance is an issue of great political significance for Europe, given the repercussions that a fully fledged US involvement — perhaps military — in the area would have on European defence strategies. Hence the almost unanimous determination of EC member countries to play a more important role in this conflict area, not only by repeated calls for negotiated solutions to the conflicts there, but by trying to contribute economically to the region's development. The amounts of economic aid involved are insignificant from the point of view of the region's needs, and by comparison with the flows of aid coming from the United States; but, given the present constraints on European finances, the decision to increase them is an important political statement.

It is on these two issues — the Falklands and Central America — that the European countries, within the framework of the EC, have reached a measure of consensus. However, at the individual level, the particular interests of European countries in Latin America differ considerably. Hence the different national approaches of each of the countries examined towards the area, the varying amount of attention they devote to it and the willingness, or lack of it, to become fully involved in Latin America in the future.

For Britain, the Falkland Islands and Belize, and the special relationship with the Commonwealth nations in the area, have been far more important than relations with the other, larger countries. However, in the wake of the Falklands conflict, Britain has sought to establish closer political relations with some of the Latin American states, especially those which were not fully supportive of Argentina and kept relatively aloof from Latin American solidarity during the conflict: namely, Mexico, Chile and Brazil.

Colonial interests have also been prominent in French relations with Latin America, especially with regard to development assistance flows, although French policy has been less complicated than that of the United Kingdom. This is mainly due to the fact that France does not have any pending territorial disputes as Britain has, and that it has successfully defused potential independentist drives by having incorporated Guadeloupe, Martinique and French Guiana into French territory in the form of Départements. French policies towards the Latin American countries have had a remarkable degree of continuity over the years, despite the changes one might have expected from the Socialists when they came to power. Apart from the breaking off of diplomatic relations with Chile, French pragmatism has continued to dominate policy, although Socialist ideology is perhaps responsible for the degree of opposition to US policies in Central America, especially Nicaragua.

Germany has been closest to Latin America, not only economically, but politically. Taking full advantage of the infrastructure offered by its transnational actors (political parties, foundations, trade unions, churches), it has maintained an active presence in Latin America which, because of its unofficial character, has established long-standing links with a wide spectrum of political parties and groups, in government and opposition. Germany has consequently managed to build up an expertise in the region's political and economic affairs that is unmatched by the other European countries.

7 Policy considerations

Until recently, Latin America did not play a significant international role. Its countries were politically introspective and highly nationalistic, and economically they strove for self-sufficiency by means of import substitution and other autarkic policies. The whole region was also largely isolated from the rest of the world because of the extent to which its external relations were dominated by the United States.

However, the Latin American economies have now become closely bound to the finance and trade of the industrial world as a whole, as their debt problems have clearly shown. Politically, too, developments in Latin América are no longer the exclusive concern of the United States. There has been widespread international interest in the democratization process in several Latin American countries, and it has also become clear that the internal political turmoil and rising tension in the region could have far-reaching consequences that may threaten international stability.

Europe can no longer afford to ignore Latin America. Nor is it in its interest to continue with *ad hoc* policies that have no consistent general direction. Indeed, if it continues with its undefined and ambiguous policies, it will at best miss out on valuable political and economic opportunities and, at worst, badly damage its existing and future interests.

Are there any real benefits that Europe could achieve from a closer relationship with Latin America? Would Latin America gain from stronger links with Europe? If the answer to these questions is positive, what steps should be taken to forge this closer relationship, bearing in mind that Europe's primary interests are still going to be centred on the industrialized world of the North, and that it is unlikely that Latin America is going to go up substantially in any European list of priorities?

There are a number of general and concrete measures and objectives in the political, economic and cultural fields which would contribute to strengthening and making better use of the existing links between Europe and Latin America; but is it reasonable to assume that they can or will be realized? Finally, would an assessment of the amount of attention and resources currently devoted to Latin America lead to the conclusion that European countries are making the best use of them?

The advantages that Europe could gain from closer links with Latin America are economic and political. Economically, it would benefit from reducing its concentration on former dependencies and diversifying its links with the Third World. Despite its present economic difficulties, Latin America is a dynamic region in terms of growth and has great potential for expansion. Several countries within the region have achieved a degree of economic development that places them well above the rest of the developing countries and suggests that they will be important international actors in the future. Brazil is already among the ten largest free-market economies and Mexico may soon be also. The region as a whole is a huge market which, given its rate of demographic and industrial growth, will become progressively more important. In the current era of fierce international commercial competition, Latin America is still a relatively untapped area. Furthermore, Europe has an advantage over the US and other industrialized countries in that Latin America feels particularly close to it and wishes to build up its economic relations.

Politically, too, closer interaction between the two regions would increase their independence from the United States and could lead to more autonomous policies in line with national interests and aspirations. Latin America is a region whose cultural and political values are very similar to those of Europe. Both regions broadly share the traditional Western liberal values of democracy and civil liberties, and they have a common political culture. It is hard to quantify the advantages of closer political links, but they are certainly as important as economic ones, and Latin America would undoubtedly benefit from them in view of its more assertive international role of late and greater autonomy from the US. During the 1970s, Latin America was active in trying to establish a New International Economic Order, but this phase of Third World activism was eventually abandoned without any major changes to the status quo, and now Europe seems to provide the most promising avenue for political cooperation.

It is fair to say that Europe, too, has become increasingly aware in the past two decades or so of the advantages to be gained from closer political ties with Latin America. In 1964 de Gaulle, in line with his unconventional style of foreign policy, made his famous two-leg tour of Latin America, visiting first Mexico and the Caribbean, and then the ten countries in South America. Italy tried to bring Latin America closer to Europe in order to ease the stress on US/Latin American relations and to achieve a greater degree of unity and security in the Western Alliance. This was the famous 'triangular' policy of 1962–5 pursued by the Italian President, Giuseppe Saragat, and his Foreign Minister, Amintore Fanfani, in which the United States, Latin America and Western Europe were to form three elements in a common security alignment.

But none of these efforts to achieve a rapprochement between the two regions, either directly or through the intermediation of the United States, had any concrete results. No doubt conditions were not ripe and there were no specific issues to work on, as well as higher priorities on each region's agenda. At this time, the early 1960s, there was a lack of support for the kind of initiatives from individual countries that the European Community is now advocating collectively. However, the international environment has changed considerably during the past twenty years. Both regions are increasing their independence from the United States; Europe is waking up to the growing importance of the Latin American market; the Latin Americans are easing their regulations on investment; and, in sum, an improved and deeper interaction between Western Europe and Latin America not only would seem much more feasible than it has been, but would be greatly beneficial to both.

Individual and collective policies

What are the issues on which a re-evaluation of policies could lead to an improvement in European relations with Latin America? In which fields could the European countries unite their efforts and co-operate in relation to Latin America, and which others are more suitable for individual initiatives?

Of the advantages that could be gained from a common approach, the most obvious is that those pronouncements or actions that are made or taken collectively by the Europeans would carry more international weight than anything said or done individually. In addition, collective and coordinated actions would create a common European framework for dealing with the region which might encourage over time a much needed continuity in policy-making. Finally, through concerted actions, Europe could adopt bolder attitudes towards the region without the fear of damaging individual bilateral relations with the United States. However, this last point could also work the other way: in order to achieve common views, the European countries might endlessly compromise until watered-down and innocuous policies towards Latin America became the norm.

In the economic field, the European countries (with the exception of Germany) have been doing less well recently than in the 1960s and 1970s, and the trends seem to indicate that they are being overtaken by a newcomer, Japan. The US, too, is recovering some ground that it had previously lost to Europe. The one consistent factor has been Europe's extensive financial exposure to the region, and perhaps a more balanced approach to Latin America, combining private commercial credits with export promotion and investment, would over the years have been more in the interest of the European countries. Of course, this would only have been possible if there had been more coordination between the economic actors involved in the region, i.e., exporters, bankers and investors. So thought should now be given to the establishment of joint commissions for furthering economic relations with Latin America in each of the European countries. Some coordination among these commissions to achieve a common framework on trade and investment policies could then be useful for finding suitable overall strategies for dealing with Latin America.

Despite the region's recent financial difficulties, Latin America presents good opportunities for European expansion. The austerity measures which came into force in the immediate aftermath of the debt crisis, as imports were cut drastically, are bound to give way in the medium and long term to a new, perhaps more selective, import drive. In the meantime, potential European exporters could make a study of which economic sectors are likely to show signs of expansion in Latin

America if the financial constraints recede, which sectors will have priority even if austere times are prolonged, and the areas in which Europe might have an advantage over other industrialized countries. Market research into potential exports to Latin America seems essential if trade with the region is going to increase. In addition, selective concentration on target countries seems a more viable strategy than spreading one's effort thinly over a greater number of states. Germany, whose trade has fared better in Latin America than that of any other European country, has concentrated on those countries with dynamic economies and larger internal markets. Britain has followed the strategy of concentrating on a few products and selling them in selected countries. This export drive has had a considerable measure of initial success and promises a sustained growth in British exports to Latin America.

Commercial relations, however, imply a two-way flow, and a long-standing grievance of Latin American countries is that European protectionism makes it difficult for them to enter the European market. Latin Americans claim that the products they could export cannot compete effectively with those of EC members' former colonies among the ACP countries, which receive preferential treatment from the EEC under the Lomé Conventions. Indeed, it has been Europe's preference for its former colonies in its development policy that has been a major source of resentment in the Latin American countries and has soured European/Latin American relations.

How justified the Latin Americans are in thinking that a Lomé-type agreement with the European Community could benefit them is open to speculation. Some have argued that the trade agreements between the ACP and the EC have been a failure, that in fact the ACP's share of EC imports fell during the period 1975-9; and that the ACP record is worse than that of developing countries as a whole. Others claim that Lomé has been very useful in helping the ACP countries to diversify their trade.[1] However, even if this last statement were accurate, a number of factors (differences in levels of development, complexity of negotiations, etc.) would seem to indicate that a convention of the Lomé type would not be the long-sought answer to improving European/Latin American commercial relations. Perhaps an overhauling and bureaucratic simplification of the Generalized System of Preferences to make it more operative, and expanding it to include a wider range of items (for example processed agricultural products), would be a better means of boosting Latin America's trade with Europe. It would certainly help to put an end to the long tradition of mutual recriminations in this field.

A *sine qua non* for improving economic and indeed political relations is to ensure that prospective traders and investors, as well as policy-makers, improve their knowledge of the region. One observation gained while researching this paper was the impressive way in which most of the interviews that took place in Germany were conducted in Spanish. Work done by Industrial Market Research Ltd on the language used by British and German export companies has revealed a similar pattern: up to 60 per cent of West German exporters negotiating sales to non-EC countries use the local language, compared with 25 to 40 per cent (depending on the region) of British companies.[2]

Similarly, a more profound knowledge of the culture, history and languages of Europe could benefit Latin America. Here the European countries' cultural diplomacy could play an important role. Cultural diplomacy as an instrument of foreign policy is not new, but its use in recent years has become more visible, as a means of exerting subtle, yet effective, influence abroad. This avenue should be further explored because, in spite of appearances, cultural diplomacy in fact also serves political, economic and ideological ends.

Apart from the common framework in which some European/ Latin American relations already take place (the CAP, the common external tariff and common initiatives such as the European Development Fund), there is another important issue on which official European collaboration could be very useful: Latin America's external debt. Because it is a problem that has had an equal effect on the major European countries, greater collaboration and coordination at the official and private level could be an effective influence in trying to reduce the possibility of the debt issue getting completely out of hand. So far collaboration has been more visible among the private banks – European, North American, Japanese – than among governments. The private banks have moved towards resolving the immediate shock of Latin America's external debt by agreeing to multiyear re-schedulings, effecting debt swaps, and by being more flexible in converting non-US banks' debt denominated in dollars to the national currency of the banks. However, the banks' *ad hoc* approaches to the debt problem will not provide the permanent solution needed. Despite repeated statements on the need to provide long-term viable strategies to defuse the 'debt bomb', nothing has yet been done to help the Latin American countries solve their financial difficulties. They will not be able to go on servicing their foreign debt on the terms and conditions negotiated up to now. Unless something is done to alleviate the terms of repayment, Latin American debt is going to remain a serious threat to the international financial system.

Despite the statements of the governments of industrialized nations at political meetings like the London Summit in 1984, nothing has materialized in the way of actions towards alleviating the debt difficulties of the less developed nations. The governments have said they intend to move in parallel with the banks over debt reschedulings, but the Paris Club has been reluctant — except in the cases of Ecuador and Costa Rica — to negotiate multiyear reschedulings of official debts. In fact, the Bonn Summit's communiqué was an illustration that the industrialized countries were less interested in the debt problems than they were a year before.

European collective action towards Latin America via the European Community, which has sought an active role in improving Europe's image in the region, has not been very successful.The channels chosen have been the dialogue with GRULA (the group of Latin American ambassadors accredited to the Community) and SELA (Sistema Económico Latinoamericano), but they have not been all that useful, and the dialogue has stalled several times. This highlights one of the clearest obstacles to improved European/Latin American relations: the EC has yet to find a common and united body it can deal with, like ASEAN for example. Several Latin American countries have completed bilateral agreements with the EC over trade and aid, but the region as a whole has not been able to put its case coherently. It is true that Latin America cannot provide overnight a united institutionalized framework with which the EC could carry out business, but proper recognition that the existing one is less than satisfactory could lead to substantial improvement. On the other hand, it is up to the EC to press for the renewal of the *ad hoc* arrangement that has existed till now, and to seek to improve institutionalized relations with Latin America.

However, even with this lack of institutional channels, there has been some notable collective action by Europe on certain issues in which it has a unifying interest. For example, the political instability in Central America, with its possible repercussions for the United States directly and the Atlantic Alliance indirectly, has become an important European concern. Moreover, European attitudes towards Central America are beginning to have a considerable influence on US/European relations. From being an area of very minor importance, Central America has entered the mainstream of European foreign policy. It is no longer an issue followed exclusively by interested individuals in important political positions (such as Régis Debray or Hans-Dietrich Genscher), but has become an area in which European political cooperation could become effective. Although different European countries hold varying views according to their political complexion, they are agreed that the problems in Central America should not be considered within the global East/West conflict, and they are all keen to encourage democratic values and regimes in the region.

What can Europe do to achieve its stated objective of easing the tensions in Central America? It has been repeatedly argued that Europe's most important role could be as a moderating influence on the United States, so that it exercises more restraint in its policy towards 'trouble' countries and groups in the region. To this end firsthand information on local developments seems indispensable. Thus, the establishment of a permanent office for the European Community on the spot, to monitor the Central American situation and report to Brussels, could be a relatively easy and inexpensive way of keeping up to date and avoiding the national bias of the accredited European diplomats in the area.

The establishment of such an office could, however, present a number of complications. Not all European countries have the same perceptions or want to become involved in the area in the same way. Those countries, therefore, with greater local interest or a desire to exert political influence in the region would probably play a dominant role and stifle genuine Community representation. The way to avoid this would be for all countries in the Community to assess their relative capacity to pursue a sustained policy towards the area and either decide to adopt full responsibility or delegate their authority to other more active and involved countries. In view of the economic constraints Europe faces, this would perhaps be the most effective use of limited funds. At the same time, the sharing of diplomatic services – the pooling of pouches for example – would enable more frequent communication between European diplomats in Latin America and their respective foreign offices, at no extra expense.

The Iberian enlargement of the European Community in 1986 presents a number of opportunities and challenges for the Community of Ten. During the negotiations over the accession of Spain and Portugal to the EC, it was argued that these countries could provide a bridge between Latin America and the Community. The bridge theory did not seem to go down well with the Latin American countries, which felt that they were developed and organized enough to be able to conduct their external relations with Europe without their former masters having to act as intermediaries. For its part, Spain seems keen on exploiting its historical advantage in *Iberoamérica* over the rest of Europe. As Fernando Morán, the Spanish Foreign Minister, asserted with reference to Central America: 'It seems obvious that Spain is the European country spiritually closest . . .'[3] Moreover, Spain attaches great importance to its accession to the EC because of its relationship with Latin America. Morán is quite explicit on this: 'Most Latin American countries now understand and support Spain's EEC membership, and it is obvious that Spain would not consider joining the EEC if it did not provide across-the-board benefits to Latin America.'[4] Such a magnanimous position invites a measure of sceptism. Will Spain's membership of the EC *per se* benefit Latin America, or will Spain's 'spiritual closeness' to Latin America be more exploitable once Spain is acting within the EC?

Once the Community has become the Twelve, it seems quite likely that EC relations will be dominated by Spain, because of its historical links, and by Germany, because of its successful economic and political penetration in recent years. If the other member countries want more balance, they will have to overcome the indifference with which they have regarded Latin America and pursue policies of their own that are appropriate to the region's importance and potential.

Any rapprochement between Europe and Latin America through a

Community approach should not — and cannot — be a substitute for bilateral policies and relations with the region and its individual states. A collective policy could never wholly satisfy the specific interests of the different European countries. However, Europe must endeavour to formulate a rational long-term policy towards Latin America if it is to do justice to one of the world's largest geographical areas.

Notes

Chapter 1

1 Enrique V. Iglesias, 'Desarrollo y equidad: El Desafío de los años ochenta', *Revista de la CEPAL*, December 1981, pp. 15–17.
2 Adalbert Krieger Vasena and Javier Pazos, *Latin America: A Broader World Role* (London: Ernest Benn, 1973), pp. 72–3; and Thomas O. Enders and Richard P. Mattione, *Latin America: The Crisis of Debt and Growth* (Washington, D.C.: The Brookings Institution, 1984), pp. 6–7.
3 Inter-American Development Bank, *Economic and Social Progress in Latin America 1984* (Washington, D.C.: IDB, 1984), p. 189.
4 Most of the trade figures in this section, unless otherwise indicated, are taken from the UNCTAD *Handbook of International Trade and Development Statistics 1983*.
5 Iglesias, 'Desarrollo y equidad', p. 18.
6 United Nations, *Yearbook of International Trade Statistics*, Vol. 1 (New York: 1984), p. 1124.
7 See, for instance, SELA, *America Latina y la Comunidad Económica Europea: Problemas y perspectivas* (Caracas: Monte Avila Editores, 1984); and 'Status of the dialogue between Latin America and the European Communities', SELA, SP/CL/X.0 DT, No. 15, 9 October 1984.
8 *Europe Documents* (Brussels: Agence Internationale d'Information pour la Presse), No. 1305, 17 April 1984, p. 3.

Chapter 2

1 On the evolution of the export credit systems in the industrialized countries, see Joan Pearce, *Subsidized Export Credit* (London: Royal Institute of International Affairs, 1980); Joan Pearce, 'Export Credit: The implications of the 1982 revision for developing countries', in Christopher Stevens, ed., *EEC and the Third World: A Survey: 3* (London: Hodder and Stoughton/ODI/IDS, 1983); and OECD, *The Export Credit Financing Systems in OECD member countries* (Paris, 1982).
2 Herbert Goldhamer, *The Foreign Powers in Latin America* (Princeton, N.J.: Princeton University Press, 1972), p. 72.

3   *Latin America Weekly Report*, 4 January 1985, p. 11.

4   Paul Betts, 'France signs Mexican deals worth FF 1.4 billion', *The Financial Times* (*FT* hereafter), 21 December 1984, p. 5.

5   *UN 1981 Yearbook of International Trade Statistics*, Vol. 1 (New York: 1982), pp. 1254, 1262.

6   'Take a long-term view of Latin America, Channon urges', *British Business*, 7 October 1983, p. 319.

7   Countertrade may adopt several forms: from barter — swap of goods — to more sophisticated varieties, including offset (an exporter transfers parts of the contract to the purchasing country); counter-purchase (the exporter undertakes to buy goods back as a proportion of his original sale); and buy-back (in which an importer of an industrial plant pays back with its output).

8   Anne Charters, 'GM Brazil opens Latin American barter drive', *FT*, 15 January 1985, p. 3.

9   *Latin America Weekly Report*, 4 January 1985.

10 Patrick Blum, 'Third World debt "forces increase in countertrading"', *FT*, 21 September 1984.

11 On the negative effects of countertrade, see Economist Intelligence Unit, *North-South Countertrade — Barter and Reciprocal Trade Agreements with Developing Countries* (London, 1984).

12 Frank Gray, 'UK banks expand countertrade activities', *FT*, 5 September 1984.

13 A historical antecedent of the expansion of trade through barter agreements in the face of lack of liquidity can be found in Germany's trade with Latin America. This had been steadily on the increase prior to World War I, but it deteriorated rapidly in the first postwar period. During the 1930s, despite the depression, Germany re-established a strong position in Latin America through barter agreements. Some countries, namely Argentina, Brazil and Chile, were able to double their exports to Germany in a relatively short period, and by 1983 Germany became the second most important trading partner for Latin America, its exports to the region being one third higher than those of Britain. Albrecht von Gleich, 'Policies toward Latin America in the Federal Republic of Germany', in Institut d'Etudes Européennes, *La Communauté Européenne et l'Amérique Latine* (Brussels: Editions de l'Université de Bruxelles, 1981), pp. 60–1.

14 *SIPRI Yearbook 1984* (London: Taylor & Francis, 1984), p. 193.

15 Frederic S. Pearson, 'The Question of Control in British Defence Sales Policy', *International Affairs*, Vol. 59, No. 2 (Spring 1983), p. 225.

16 SIPRI, *The Arms Trade with the Third World* (Stockholm & New York: Almqvist & Wilsell, Humanities Press, 1971), p. 253.

17 E. A. Koldoziej, 'French Arms Trade: The Economic Determinants', in *SIPRI Yearbook 1983* (London: Taylor & Francis, 1983), p. 372.

18 *Ibid.*, p. 383.

19 *SIPRI Yearbook 1984*, p. 231.
20 *Ibid.*, p. 376.
21 SIPRI, *The Arms Trade with the Third World*, p. 255.
22 An average of 14 per cent for the aggregate 1966–79, and 17 per cent in 1973–7. Although the average dropped to a record low in 1976, it rose to 33 per cent in 1977, 13 per cent in 1978, and 22 per cent in 1979. Pearson, *op. cit.*, p. 219, Table 2A.
23 A good survey of potential conflicts in the region and their causes is found in Jack Child, *Geopolitics and Conflict in South America* (New York: Praeger, 1985).
24 *Latin America Weekly Report*, 15 January 1982, and 5 February 1982.
25 *Ibid.*, 29 January 1982.
26 'British readiness to sell arms to Chile regime alarms US', *The Times*, 21 February 1983.
27 *SIPRI Yearbook 1984*, p. 190.

Chapter 3

1 In the case of the UK, the two concepts of operational importance are the Aid Programme and the Public Expenditure on Overseas Aid (PE). The former is the official budget for overseas aid administered by the Overseas Development Administration (ODA). The latter, PE, does not include expenditure by the Export Credits Guarantee Department (ECGD), but does include contributions to multilateral lending agencies (i.e. the International Development Association and Regional Development Banks).
2 Participation of the three countries in overall oda within the DAC in 1982 was 6.4 per cent for the UK, 11.3 per cent for Germany and 14.3 per cent for France, compared with 10.8 per cent and 29.7 per cent for Japan and the US respectively: OECD, *Development Cooperation 1983 Review* (Paris, 1983), p. 76.
3 Full text in OECD, *Development Cooperation 1984 Review* p. 71.
4 Overseas Development Administration, *British Aid Statistics 1979–1983*, p. xiv; OECD, *Development Cooperation 1984 Review*, (Paris, 1984), p. 71.
5 'The case against bilateral aid', *FT*, 1 August 1984.
6 Hassam M. Selim, *Development Assistance Policies and the Performance of Aid Agencies* (London: Macmillan, 1983), p. 101.
7 OECD, *Development Cooperation 1983 Review* (Paris, 1983), p. 68.
8 *Latin America Weekly Report*, 17 August 1984, p. 6.
9 In 1980 Africa received 36 per cent of the total, followed by Asia with 28 per cent, Europe with 18 per cent and Latin America with 12 per cent: OECD, *Development Cooperation 1981 Review* (Paris, 1981), p. 99.
10 *Latin America Weekly Report*, 17 August 1984.

11 'Bonn aid for El Salvador', *FT*, 18 July 1984, p. 47.
12 *Latin America Weekly Report*, 17 August 1984, p. 7.
13 On the split between bureaucratic units on policies towards developing countries, see Barbara B. Crane, 'Policy coordination by major western powers in bargaining with the Third World: debt relief and the Common Fund', *International Organization*, Vol. 38, No. 3 (Summer 1984), 399–428.
14 Vincent Cable, *British Interests and Third World Development* (London: Overseas Development Institute, 1980), p. 15.
15 'Aid in the age of Raison', *Guardian*, 13 July 1984.
16 *Ibid.*
17 OECD, *Development Cooperation 1983 Review*; *FT*, 1 August 1984. This can be explained by the fact that multilateral commitments are difficult to cut down, but with a reduced budget bilateral aid shows a decline.
18 The deal, worth £380 million, was arranged on a government-to-government basis and signed during Mrs Thatcher's visit to Mexico to attend the Cancún summit. The aid grant was criticized in Britain at the time, since it entailed £195 million in the form of export credits on very favourable interest terms.
19 Jean-Pierre Cot, 'Winning East–West in North–South', *Foreign Policy*, No. 46 (Spring 1982), p. 4.
20 Quoted in Yves Berthelot and D. Besnaiou, 'France's new Third World policy: problems of change', in Stevens, ed., *EEC and the Third World: A Survey: 3*, p. 34.
21 *Ibid.*
22 Jean-Pierre Cot, *A l'épreuve du pouvoir* (Paris: Editions du Seuil, 1984), pp. 20, 38.

Chapter 4

1 United Nations, *Salient Features and Trends in Foreign Direct Investment* (New York, 1983), p. 15.
2 *Ibid.*, p. 17.
3 Hassan M. Selim, *Development Assistance Policies and the Performance of Aid Agencies* (London: Macmillan, 1983), p. 105.
4 OECD, *Development Cooperation 1980 Review* (Paris, 1980), p. 164.
5 A comprehensive account of this is found in Charles Oman, *New Forms of International Investment in Developing Countries* (Paris: OECD Development Centre Studies, 1984).
6 *Latin America Weekly Report*, 4 January 1985; Hugh O'Shaughnessy, 'Latin America eases way for investors', *FT*, 12 December 1984, p. 4.
7 Bernard A. Lietaer, *Europe + Latin America + the Multinationals* (Farnborough: Saxon House, 1979), p. 21.
8 Francisco Valdés Treviño and Carlos F. Molina del Pozo, *La inversión de la Comunidad Europea y de España en México*

(Universidad Autónoma de Nuevo León, 1983), p. 79 and Table 2 in the Appendix.
9 Figures from the Banco Nacional de Comercio Exterior (Mexico, December 1984).
10 OECD, *Internaional Direct Investment Trends* (Paris, 1981), p. 70, Table 21.
11 *Latin America Weekly Report*, 23 November 1983.

Chapter 5

1 CEPAL, *Balance preliminar de la economía Latinoamericana en 1984* (Santiago, January 1985), p. 16.
2 William Hall, 'The small banks get nervous', *FT*, 21 December 1982.
3 Banco de México, *Informe Hacendario Mensual*, No. 1 (May 1983), p. 25.
4 'Feldstein says banks should cut rates on loans to Third World', *International Herald Tribune*, 25 February 1983.
5 David Lascelles, 'UK will not reschedule official loans to Mexico', *FT*, 3 September 1984, p. 3; 'A debt promise unfulfilled', *FT*, 10 January 1985, p. 12.

Chapter 6

1 It could be argued that the East Asian NICs have outperformed the Latin American countries economically. However, the NICs' impressive growth rates are relatively recent, and as countries they are not quite comparable with Latin American ones. Hong Kong and Singapore are city-states, while South Korea and Taiwan for political reasons have in fact become US protegés.
2 American opposition to the German/Brazilian nuclear deal can be regarded as the exception in economic relations. Although it was argued that American objections were related to security considerations, a more plausible explanation was the need to defend US industrialists in an industry characterized by intense international competition.
3 See Trevor Taylor, *European Defence Cooperation*, Chatham House Paper No. 24 (London: RIIA/Routledge & Kegan Paul, 1984).
4 Philip Webster, 'Mrs Thatcher comes off the fence', *The Times*, 31 October 1983.
5 An example of this was the tone of the political debate in the UK, for instance: 'Parliament: Dual key rejected: US trusts us so we should trust them', *The Times*, 1 November 1983, p. 4.
6 On the extent of American logistical support for Britain, see *The Economist*, 3 March 1984, pp. 23–5.
7 James M. Markham, 'Reagan's moves in Central America make Atlantic partners uneasy', *International Herald Tribune*,

3 August 1983 (italics in the original).

8 See, for instance, Stuart Holland and Donald Anderson, *Kissinger's Kingdom?* (Nottingham: Russell Press, 1984).

9 David Ronfeldt, *Geopolitics, Security and US Strategy in the Caribbean Basin* (Santa Monica: Rand, 1983), pp. 33–4.

10 The independentist drive in New Caledonia and French responses to this challenge may have some 'demonstration effect' on the French DOM in the Western hemisphere and perhaps lead to a re-evaluation of French colonial policy.

11 Herbert Goldhamer, *The Foreign Powers in Latin America* (Santa Monica/Princeton, N.J.: The Rand Corporation/Princeton University Press, 1972), p. 7.

12 Nicole Bourdillat, 'La Politique Latinoaméricaine de la France', in Institut d'Etudes Européennes, *La Communauté Européenne et L'Amérique Latine*, p. 35.

13 'And we end up by pushing to the opposite camp peoples who are not natural adversaries of the West but they become so by the logic of the situation we impose on them.' Interview with François Mitterrand, *Time*, 19 October 1981, quoted in Michel Tatu, 'La position française: les difficultés d'être un bon "Latino"', *Politique Etrangère*, Vol. 2 (1982), p. 320.

14 Jonathan Marcus and Bruce George, 'The ambiguous consensus: French defence policy under Mitterrand', *The World Today*, October 1983.

15 Colin Henfrey and Liz Nash, '"Business as usual": Britain's Tory government and Latin America', in Latin America Bureau, *Europe and Latin America* (London: Latin America Bureau, 1980), p. 12.

16 *Franks Report* (London: HMSO, Cmnd 8787, 1983), para. 22.

17 House of Commons, Fifth Report from the Foreign Affairs Committee Session 1983–1984, *Falkland Islands Report*, Vol. 1, para. 29.

18 Dieter W. Benecke, Michael Domitra *et al.*, *The Relations between the Federal Republic of Germany and Latin America* (Bonn: Friedrich Ebert Stiftung, 1984), p. 6.

19 Although the British and French Socialist parties also belong to the SI, they have not been active to the same extent as the German SPD in using this channel to pursue political interests in Latin America.

Chapter 7

1 See, for instance, Christopher Stevens and Ann Weston, 'Trade Diversification: Has Lomé Helped?', in Christopher Stevens, ed., *EEC and the Third World: A Survey: 4* (London: Hodder & Stoughton/ODI/IDS, 1984).

2 Industrial Market Research Ltd, *How British and German Industry Exports* (London, 1978), p. vi.

3 Fernando Morán, 'Europe's Role in Central America: A Spanish Socialist View', in Andrew J. Pierre, ed., *Third World Instability: Central America as a European-American Issue* (New York: Council on Foreign Relations, 1985), p. 35.
4 *Ibid.*, p. 43.